DR. LEE ANN B. MARINO, PH.D., D.MIN., D.D.

DISCOVERING INTIMACY

A Journey
Through the Song of Solomon

DISCOVERING INTIMACY
A Journey Through the Song of Solomon

DR. LEE ANN B. MARINO, PH.D., D.MIN., D.D.

Published by:

Righteous Pen Publications
(An imprint of the Righteous Pen Publications Group)
www.righteouspenpublications.com

Cover and interior photos are in the Public Domain.

Book Classification: Books > Religion & Spirituality > Christian Books & Bibles > Bible Study & Reference > Commentaries > Old Testament > Poetry & Wisdom Literature.

Books > Religion & Spirituality > Christian Books & Bibles > Christian Living > Marriage.

ISBN: 1-940197-23-6
13-Digit: 978-1940197-23-4

Printed in the United States of America.

And I can feel you breathe,
it's washing over me
And suddenly I'm melting into you
There's nothing left to prove
And baby, all we need is just to be

Caught up in the touch, slow and steady rush
Baby, isn't that the way
That love's supposed to be?
I can feel you breathe, just breathe

- Faith Hill, Breathe

TABLE OF CONTENTS

AUTHOR'S NOTE

As of the revision of this book, I have published over 35 manuscripts and written close to 50. While I have written on many topics, the majority of what I have written is predominately instructional. This also reflects most of my ministry work, which revolves around the educational and leadership training aspects of my ministry. So, when I decided to do this commentary on the Song of Solomon, I figured it would follow in course like most of my other writings, spanning nearly fifteen years of text and direction.

When I attempted to write in my usual manner with this book, I found myself unable to write and frequently frustrated. I felt like I was unable to convey what I truly wanted to convey. The text seemed to be missing something – a disconnect, if you will – in its purpose. This reality proved both frustrating and intriguing, forcing me to examine the matter more carefully and consider just how to piece this work together so it would both make sense and convey its purpose to the reader.

When writing Biblical commentaries, it is typical to either comment on every single verse or group the verses by paragraph and comment on every single theme in the written order in which they appear. When I started this commentary on the Song of Solomon, I attempted to do this, following the orthodox format for commentary writing. In doing so, I hit multiple challenges in the execution of the work. I found it to be either exceedingly redundant or confusing. I also grew frustrated as I reached chapter 4 and seemed to be out of ideas that would run concurrent with the text.

Seeking advice, I forwarded what I had of chapter 4 onto another writer, my long-time friend Aaron Joy, who gave me the advice to reassess what I had written. I knew what I had was not the greatest and I needed to go in another direction. The result of that different direction was a lot of work, but an overall better product that I am more pleased with than I was with the original version of this manuscript.

The major challenge I faced was how to create a commentary based on prose and poetry, one that conveys different ideas in each stanza that may – or may not – have much (on the surface) to do with whatever content goes before or after it. The solution was, therefore, to handle this commentary differently, dividing up the ideas and principles in a manner not customary for commentaries. To bring a sense of order and practicality, it's not possible to comment on it verse-by-verse or even chapter-by-chapter. My attempts to do that caused the work to be rambling and disorganized. The Song of Solomon is not a book that can be understood in a dry reading of the text. It is lyrically written; it is a poem, a love song, an expression of intimacy that must be understood by its thematic content. To convey this, we first have the Song of Solomon in its complete eight-chapter rendering. From there, the chapters of this book are divided up by theme, expressing key insights into the contents of this book. For these chapters, we will review verses and passages that relate to these themes and see how it all comes together in the beauty of intimacy. The result is a more coherent work, one that does not seek to derive the same points in different ways from the same strains of repeated thought.

Lastly, this commentary has become to me more than just a commentary: it is also the result of my own discoveries about the different issues that surround intimacy and the way those issues affected my own life. As I worked on this book, I realized the patterns in my own life that impacted connections I have with others. I have discovered it is who we connect to rather than avoiding connection all together, which I have been tempted to do at times. The result was an intense battle, a struggle, that

I believe I have gone through to prepare for what is next in my life. Do I have it all figured out? No, I don't. God's work within us is often progressive and comes with the unfolding of time. We understand it more in hindsight than foresight, and things seem much clearer later than they do right now. The glass we see through darkly (1 Corinthians 13:12) forces the faith we must pursue as we are challenged to connect to others, pushing through the results of sin to embrace all God has for us both this side of heaven and in the greater scheme of eternity. As He reveals, I move with Him.

I do know that from doing this study on a most overlooked book of Scripture, presenting this writing, and now revising it, I have a better idea of what I need, what I seek, and yes, what I will find in my relationship with God and others...and I am ready for that, be it in ministry, be it personal, be it professional, whatever, however, and whenever it may be.

INTRODUCTION

About the Song of Solomon

W hat does the Bible teach us about intimacy…and why? How does God illustrate intimacy? Why is intimacy important, both between people and in our relationship with God? How is such expressed? How does the Bible approach sexual attraction? Even though you have most likely never heard a message from the Song of Solomon, this book answers all the questions posed above. The overt and underlying theme of the Song of Solomon is intimacy. In its contents, we learn about the nature of intimacy and how it changes us as people. For this reason, the Song of Solomon is essential for believers, both in this age, and every age. It is a type and a reality: it describes intimacy between people and is also a type of the relationship between Christ and His Church, God and His people. In studying the Song of Solomon, we walk away with eight key understandings:

- A visual understanding of intimacy and the importance it plays in the life of the believer.

- The relevance of intimacy in interpersonal relationships and our relationship with God.

- The dynamics of intimate relationships.

- The ideal intimacy present in a marriage relationship that is appointed by God and established for His glory.

- Things that disrupt intimacy in a relationship, and the reason such disruptions are often detrimental to an intimate balance.

- Ways to guard and support intimacy in relationships.

- Seeing the spiritual principle behind intimacy.

- Seeing the Song of Solomon as both a type and a reality: it is a type of the relationship, the intimacy between Christ and the church, and God and His people, and also the reality of intimacy which should exist between spouses, as a type of Christ and the church.

Identity

Depending on the translation one uses, the Song of Solomon may also be known as the Canticle of Canticles, Song of Songs, the High Song, or the Ultimate Song. In the Hebrew, its title is in the superlative, indicating that it is the most perfect, excellent, and complete of all songs. This tells us that its contents, while describing something between people, is describing the ultimate of something spiritual.

Position in the Bible

The Song of Solomon is in a group of eleven writings classified as just that – the "Writings." Within the "Writings" there are three classifications of books: The Poetic Books, The Five Scrolls, and Other Books. The Song of Solomon classifies as both poetic and is included in The

Five Scrolls, along with Ruth, Lamentations, Ecclesiastes, and Esther. These are classified due to their late inclusion in the Biblical canon, of dispute until around the 2nd century B.C. Depending on the translation used, the Song of Solomon may have two possible positions: it either follows the book of Ecclesiastes and precedes the book of Isaiah or follows the book of Job and precedes the book of Ruth.

Length

The Song of Solomon is one of the shortest books in the Bible, consisting in total of only 117 verses. It is eight chapters long. Even in Bibles that sometimes number the verses differently, the Song of Solomon remains eight chapters, and the content is the same.

Author

The Song of Solomon is commonly attributed to Solomon as the author. In some traditions, the book is attributed as being written by God, through Solomon. This is not, however, without debate. It is possible the song is addressed to Solomon as the audience of the song, rather than being authored by Solomon. Some attribute it to a different grammatical structure than present during the time of Solomon, and therefore, dating it to a time and place other than Solomon's era. This would classify the writing as pseudepigrapha, a word meaning "false authorship." In this case, the author was most likely an unknown who wrote under Solomon's name to give the writing credibility. The practice of pseudepigraphic writing was very common in ancient times and takes nothing away from the content or inspiration of the text.

About the author

If Solomon is the author of the Song of Solomon, we know

him to be David's son, the King of Israel. Solomon became co-regent with his father for the last three years of David's reign and was then King of Israel. He was the last king of Israel to serve before the kingdom of Israel split into two kingdoms. Solomon was known to have over three hundred wives and seven hundred concubines, which causes many to question the legitimacy of Solomon's authorship of the Song of Songs. Since Solomon's relationships were often political alliances, it is unlikely he loved the women he was with. We can consider, however, that it may refer to a special relationship or marriage he may have had at some point in his life. If the author is unknown, we obviously do not know anything about them.

What we can see in the Song of Solomon is a uniquely female perspective to relationships. Rather than exclusively male-dominated, as was common in literature of that time, the Song of Solomon shows a woman as equally interested in a relationship and pursuant to that of a man. Her expressions of intimacy are as vivid and erotic as his, which gives us an important look into God's concept of male-female relationships. Rather than having a male perspective with a male-dominated pursuer, the relationship appears equal and equally pursuant one to another. Whoever authored this book had a clear concept and picture into a woman's desires within a relationship.

Time written

Nobody is exactly sure when the Song of Solomon was written. If it was written during Solomon's lifetime, that would put it somewhere between 1000 and 900 B.C. Due to the language of the text, some suggest it was written later, around the fifth century B.C.

Who is the Song of Solomon for?

The Song of Solomon is a book for all believers. It holds relevance, truth, and teaching that can be applied to every believer's circumstance throughout their lives. It also holds a special relevance for Christian believers who are married or are preparing for marriage.

As the Song of Solomon is also a powerful instruction in intimacy, the book provides us the basics in intimate relationships, both with God and one another.

History

The exact history of the Song of Solomon is debated. Those who credit Solomon as the author or the work written for Solomon believe it was written during Solomon's lifetime. A study of the language present in the work divides the era of its writing. Some suggest it was written somewhere around 900 B.C., while others suggest the language indicates the postexilic period (the fifth century B.C.). The discrepancy in time is, therefore, approximately four hundred years. Aside from study of the language involved, the text itself does not give us any indication of the time in which it was written. Its themes apply to a variety of ages and its underlying theme of love and relationship spans time and space right down to the present day. In many ways, its contents represent dynamics that are eternal.

Throughout history, the question of the canonization of the Song of Solomon has been disputed. It was one of the last books of the Old Testament to be canonized. Both Martin Luther and John Calvin felt it inappropriate in the Bible. There are still people who consider the work to be too "feminine" in nature or consider its overtly sexual content to be wrong for God's Word. To this very day, the Church of Jesus Christ of Latter-Day Saints rejects the work as non-canonical and uninspired.

Context

The Song of Solomon is presented as a discourse. The major narratives within the book are the woman (sometimes described as the Shulamite woman) and the man. Neither are ever named within the dialogue.

The Song of Solomon is unique among books for two things. The first is a sexual dynamic. The love presented between the characters is often spoken of in the language of physical attraction and dynamic. Underneath that dynamic we find something powerful: an intimacy between the two. It provides a unique sense of love and commitment, a true fidelity between partners. The intensity in the book shows forth the love that should exist between those in relationship whom God has joined together in marriage. It also shows the intense love that exists between God and His people, an intimacy to exist between those who believe in God and God Himself.

The Song of Solomon is also unique for its powerful look into intimacy. This book expounds and defies convention and culture for the sake of true intimacy. In the presence of intimacy, the need for the law, for numerous rules and regulations, and the need to have everything defined fades away. The powerful poetic recitation of the song gives us a deeper sense of its beauty and the dance that exists within intimacy and the important discovery of it for us with other people and with God in our lives.

SECTION I

The Song of Solomon

Chapter 1

Solomon's Song of Songs.

Beloved

Let him kiss me with the kisses of his mouth—
for your love is more delightful than wine.
Pleasing is the fragrance of your perfumes;
your name is like perfume poured out.
No wonder the maidens love you!
Take me away with you—let us hurry!
Let the king bring me into his chambers.

Friends

We rejoice and delight in you;
we will praise your love more than wine.

Beloved

How right they are to adore you!
Dark am I, yet lovely,
O daughters of Jerusalem,
dark like the tents of Kedar,
like the tent curtains of Solomon.
Do not stare at me because I am dark,
because I am darkened by the sun.
My mother's sons were angry with me
and made me take care of the vineyards;
my own vineyard I have neglected.
Tell me, you whom I love, where you graze
your flock and where you rest your sheep at midday.
Why should I be like a veiled woman
beside the flocks of your friends?

Friends

If you do not know, most beautiful of women,
follow the tracks of the sheep
and graze your young goats
by the tents of the shepherds.

Lover

I liken you, my darling, to a mare
harnessed to one of the chariots of
Pharaoh.
Your cheeks are beautiful with earrings,
your neck with strings of jewels.
We will make you earrings of gold,
studded with silver.

Beloved

While the king was at his table,
my perfume spread its fragrance.
My lover is to me a sachet of myrrh
resting between my breasts.
My lover is to me a cluster of henna blossoms
from the vineyards of En Gedi.

Lover

How beautiful you are, my darling!
Oh, how beautiful!
Your eyes are doves.

Beloved

How handsome you are, my lover!
Oh, how charming!
And our bed is verdant.

Lover

The beams of our house are cedars;
our rafters are firs.

Chapter 2

Beloved

I am a rose of Sharon,
a lily of the valleys.

Lover

Like a lily among thorns
is my darling among the maidens.

Beloved

Like an apple tree among the trees of the forest
is my lover among the young men.
I delight to sit in his shade,
and his fruit is sweet to my taste.
He has taken me to the banquet hall,
and his banner over me is love.
Strengthen me with raisins,
refresh me with apples,
for I am faint with love.
His left arm is under my head,
and his right arm embraces me.
Daughters of Jerusalem, I charge you
by the gazelles and by the does of the field:
Do not arouse or awaken love until it so desires.

Listen! My lover!
Look! Here he comes,
leaping across the mountains,
bounding over the hills.
My lover is like a gazelle or a young stag.
Look! There he stands behind our wall,
gazing through the windows,
peering through the lattice.

My lover spoke and said to me,
"Arise, my darling,
my beautiful one, and come with me.
See! The winter is past;
the rains are over and gone.
Flowers appear on the earth;
the season of singing has come,
the cooing of doves
is heard in our land.
The fig tree forms its early fruit;
the blossoming vines spread their fragrance.
Arise, come, my darling;
my beautiful one, come with me."

Lover

My dove in the clefts of the rock,
in the hiding places on the mountainside,
show me your face,
let me hear your voice;
for your voice is sweet,
and your face is lovely.
Catch for us the foxes,
the little foxes that ruin the vineyards,
our vineyards that are in bloom.

Beloved

My lover is mine and I am his;
he browses among the lilies.
Until the day breaks
and the shadows flee,
turn, my lover,
and be like a gazelle
or like a young stag
on the rugged hills.

Chapter 3

All night long on my bed
I looked for the one my heart loves;
I looked for him but did not find him.
I will get up now and go about the city,
through its streets and squares;
I will search for the one my heart loves.
So I looked for him but did not find him.
The watchmen found me
as they made their rounds in the city.
"Have you seen the one my heart loves?"
Scarcely had I passed them
when I found the one my heart loves.
I held him and would not let him go
till I had brought him to my mother's house,
to the room of the one who conceived me.
Daughters of Jerusalem, I charge you
by the gazelles and by the does of the field:
Do not arouse or awaken love
until it so desires.
Who is this coming up from the desert
like a column of smoke,
perfumed with myrrh and incense
made from all the spices of the merchant?
Look! It is Solomon's carriage,
escorted by sixty warriors,
the noblest of Israel,
all of them wearing the sword,
all experienced in battle,
each with his sword at his side,
prepared for the terrors of the night.
King Solomon made for himself the carriage;
he made it of wood from Lebanon.
Its posts he made of silver,
its base of gold.
Its seat was upholstered with purple,

its interior lovingly inlaid
by the daughters of Jerusalem.
Come out, you daughters of Zion,
and look at King Solomon wearing the crown,
the crown with which his mother crowned him
on the day of his wedding,
the day his heart rejoiced.

Chapter 4

Lover

How beautiful you are, my darling!
Oh, how beautiful!
Your eyes behind your veil are doves.
Your hair is like a flock of goats
descending from Mount Gilead.
Your teeth are like a flock of sheep just shorn,
coming up from the washing.
Each has its twin;
not one of them is alone.
Your lips are like a scarlet ribbon;
your mouth is lovely.
Your temples behind your veil
are like the halves of a pomegranate.
Your neck is like the tower of David,
built with elegance;
on it hang a thousand shields,
all of them shields of warriors.
Your two breasts are like two fawns,
like twin fawns of a gazelle
that browse among the lilies.
Until the day breaks
and the shadows flee,
I will go to the mountain of myrrh
and to the hill of incense.
All beautiful you are, my darling;
there is no flaw in you.

Come with me from Lebanon, my bride,
come with me from Lebanon.
Descend from the crest of Amana,
from the top of Senir, the summit of Hermon,
from the lions' dens
and the mountain haunts of the leopards.

You have stolen my heart, my sister, my bride;
you have stolen my heart
with one glance of your eyes,
with one jewel of your necklace.
How delightful is your love, my sister, my bride!
How much more pleasing is your love than wine,
and the fragrance of your perfume than any spice!
Your lips drop sweetness as the honeycomb, my bride;
milk and honey are under your tongue.
The fragrance of your garments is like that of Lebanon.
You are a garden locked up, my sister, my bride;
you are a spring enclosed, a sealed fountain.
Your plants are an orchard of pomegranates
with choice fruits,
with henna and nard,
nard and saffron,
calamus and cinnamon,
with every kind of incense tree,
with myrrh and aloes
and all the finest spices.
You are a garden fountain,
a well of flowing water
streaming down from Lebanon.

Beloved

Awake, north wind,
and come, south wind!
Blow on my garden,
that its fragrance may spread abroad.
Let my lover come into his garden
and taste its choice fruits.

Chapter 5

Lover

I have come into my garden, my sister, my bride;
I have gathered my myrrh with my spice.
I have eaten my honeycomb and my honey;
I have drunk my wine and my milk.

Friends

Eat, O friends, and drink;
Drink your fill, O lovers.

Beloved

I slept but my heart was awake.
Listen! My lover is knocking:
"Open to me, my sister, my darling,
my dove, my flawless one.
My head is drenched with dew,
my hair with the dampness of the night."
I have taken off my robe—
must I put it on again?
I have washed my feet—
must I soil them again?
My lover thrust his hand through the latch-opening;
my heart began to pound for him.
I arose to open for my lover,
and my hands dripped with myrrh,
my fingers with flowing myrrh,
on the handles of the lock.
I opened for my lover,
but my lover had left; he was gone.
My heart sank at his departure.
I looked for him but did not find him.
I called him but he did not answer.

The watchmen found me
as they made their rounds in the city.
They beat me, they bruised me;
they took away my cloak,
those watchmen of the walls!
O daughters of Jerusalem, I charge you—
if you find my lover,
what will you tell him?
Tell him I am faint with love.

Friends

How is your beloved better than others,
most beautiful of women?
How is your beloved better than others,
that you charge us so?

Beloved

My lover is radiant and ruddy,
outstanding among ten thousand.
His head is purest gold;
his hair is wavy
and black as a raven.
His eyes are like doves
by the water streams,
washed in milk,
mounted like jewels.
His cheeks are like beds of spice
yielding perfume.
His lips are like lilies
dripping with myrrh.
His arms are rods of gold
set with chrysolite.
His body is like polished ivory
decorated with sapphires.
His legs are pillars of marble
set on bases of pure gold.

His appearance is like Lebanon,
choice as its cedars.
His mouth is sweetness itself;
he is altogether lovely.
This is my lover, this my friend,
O daughters of Jerusalem.

Chapter 6

Friends

Where has your lover gone,
most beautiful of women?
Which way did your lover turn,
that we may look for him with you?

Beloved

My lover has gone down to his garden,
to the beds of spices,
to browse in the gardens
and to gather lilies.
I am my lover's and my lover is mine;
he browses among the lilies.

Lover

You are beautiful, my darling, as Tirzah,
lovely as Jerusalem,
majestic as troops with banners.
Turn your eyes from me;
they overwhelm me.
Your hair is like a flock of goats
descending from Gilead.
Your teeth are like a flock of sheep
coming up from the washing.
Each has its twin,
not one of them is alone.
Your temples behind your veil
are like the halves of a pomegranate.
Sixty queens there may be,
and eighty concubines,
and virgins beyond number;
but my dove, my perfect one, is unique,

the only daughter of her mother,
the favorite of the one who bore her.
The maidens saw her and called her blessed;
the queens and concubines praised her.

Friends

Who is this that appears like the dawn,
fair as the moon, bright as the sun,
majestic as the stars in procession?

Lover

I went down to the grove of nut trees
to look at the new growth in the valley,
to see if the vines had budded
or the pomegranates were in bloom.
Before I realized it,
my desire set me among the royal chariots of
my people.

Friends

Come back, come back, O Shulammite;
come back, come back, that we may gaze
on you!

Lover

Why would you gaze on the Shulammite
as on the dance of Mahanaim.

Chapter 7

How beautiful your sandaled feet,
O prince's daughter!
Your graceful legs are like jewels,
the work of a craftsman's hands.
Your navel is a rounded goblet
that never lacks blended wine.
Your waist is a mound of wheat
encircled by lilies.
Your breasts are like two fawns,
twins of a gazelle.
Your neck is like an ivory tower.
Your eyes are the pools of Heshbon
by the gate of Bath Rabbim.
Your nose is like the tower of Lebanon
looking toward Damascus.
Your head crowns you like Mount Carmel.
Your hair is like royal tapestry;
the king is held captive by its tresses.
How beautiful you are and how pleasing,
O love, with your delights!
Your stature is like that of the palm,
and your breasts like clusters of fruit.
I said, "I will climb the palm tree;
I will take hold of its fruit."
May your breasts be like the clusters of the
vine,
the fragrance of your breath like apples,
and your mouth like the best wine.

Beloved

May the wine go straight to my lover,
flowing gently over lips and teeth.
I belong to my lover,
and his desire is for me.

Come, my lover, let us go to the countryside,
let us spend the night in the villages.
Let us go early to the vineyards
to see if the vines have budded,
if their blossoms have opened,
and if the pomegranates are in bloom—
there I will give you my love.
The mandrakes send out their fragrance,
and at our door is every delicacy,
both new and old,
that I have stored up for you, my lover.

Chapter 8

If only you were to me like a brother,
who was nursed at my mother's breasts!
Then, if I found you outside,
I would kiss you,
and no one would despise me.
I would lead you
and bring you to my mother's house—
she who has taught me.
I would give you spiced wine to drink,
the nectar of my pomegranates.
His left arm is under my head
and his right arm embraces me.
Daughters of Jerusalem, I charge you:
Do not arouse or awaken love
until it so desires.

Friends

Who is this coming up from the desert
leaning on her lover?

Beloved

Under the apple tree I roused you;
there your mother conceived you,
there she who was in labor gave you birth.
Place me like a seal over your heart,
like a seal on your arm;
for love is as strong as death,
its jealousy unyielding as the grave.
It burns like blazing fire,
like a mighty flame.
Many waters cannot quench love;
rivers cannot wash it away.
If one were to give

all the wealth of his house for love,
it would be utterly scorned.

Friends

We have a young sister,
and her breasts are not yet grown.
What shall we do for our sister
for the day she is spoken for?
If she is a wall,
we will build towers of silver on her.
If she is a door,
we will enclose her with panels of cedar.

Beloved

I am a wall,
and my breasts are like towers.
Thus I have become in his eyes
like one bringing contentment.
Solomon had a vineyard in Baal Hamon;
he let out his vineyard to tenants.
Each was to bring for its fruit
a thousand shekels of silver.
But my own vineyard is mine to give;
the thousand shekels are for you, O Solomon,
and two hundred are for those who tend its fruit.

Lover

You who dwell in the gardens
with friends in attendance,
let me hear your voice!

Beloved

Come away, my lover,
and be like a gazelle

or like a young stag
on the spice-laden mountains.

SECTION II

The Commentary

CHAPTER 1

Beyond the Superficial

Key verses

- **Verse 3:5:** *"Daughters of Jerusalem, I charge you by the gazelles and by the does of the field: Do not arouse or awaken love until it so desires."*

- **Verses 4:9-10:** *"You have stolen my heart, my sister, my bride; you have stolen my heart with one glance of your eyes, with one jewel of your necklace. How delightful is your love, my sister, my bride! How much more pleasing is your love than wine, and the fragrance of your perfume than any spice!*

- **Verses 5:2-4:** *I slept but my heart was awake. Listen! My lover is knocking: "Open to me, my sister, my darling, my dove, my flawless one. My head is drenched with dew, my hair with the dampness of the night." I have taken off my robe-- must I put it on again? I have washed my feet-- must I soil them again? My lover thrust his hand through the latch-opening; my heart began to pound for him.*

Words and phrases to know

- **Song of Songs:** From the Hebrew word *shiyr* two times together, which means a double "song."[1]

- **Bed:** From the Hebrew word *mishkab* which means "lying down, couch, bier, act of lying."[2]

- **Search:** From the Hebrew word *baqash* which means "to seek, require, desire, exact, request."[3]

- **Watchmen:** From the Hebrew word *shamar* which means "to keep, guard, observe, give heed"[4]

- **Held:** From the Hebrew word "'achaz" which means "grasp, take hold, seize, take possession."[5]

- **Arouse and awaken:** From the Hebrew word *'uwr* which means "to rouse oneself, awake, awaken, excite."[6]

- **Love:** From the Hebrew word *'ahabah* which means "love; God's love to His people."[7]

- **Desires:** From the Hebrew word *chaphets* which means "to delight in, take pleasure in, desire, be pleased with; to move, bend down."[8]

- **Lover:** From the Hebrew word *dowd* or *dod* which means "beloved, love, uncle."[9]

- **Myrrh:** From the Hebrew word: *more* or *mowr* which means "myrrh"[10]

- **Bride:** From the Hebrew word *kallah* which means "bride, daughter-in-law."[11]

- **Stolen my heart:** From the Hebrew word *labab* which means "to ravish, become intelligent, get a mind; to make cakes, bake cakes, cook bread."[12]

- **Pleasing:** From the Hebrew word *towb* which means "to be good, be pleasing, be joyful, be beneficial, be pleasant, be favorable, be happy, be right."[13]

It's no secret: we live in a superficial world. Many people think ideal beauty is found in rail-thin, air-brushed models. Many people have the impression that pornographic images are a realistic and desirable ideal for intimate relationships. Some still insist love and faithfulness can start as hooking up on random dating sites. Commitment and long-term relationships are considered outdated, something from a bygone era that our grandparents speak of in misty-eyed memories. Many couples that stay together for long periods of time claim to be happy on the surface, but realities of infidelity, anger, hostility, and lack of love pervade their lives.

Modern-day advice about relationships takes a variety of forms, but just about all of it has one main thing in common: it emphasizes, rather than de-emphasizes, the superficial aspects of human interaction. Relationship advice tends to be a stiff rendering of dos and don'ts, reducing men and women to a series of roles. We are told, if we will only do this, this, and this, we will be happy in our relationship. Men are supposed to make money, women are supposed to spend it. Men are supposed to be tough and unfeeling, and women are supposed to be soft and over-emotional. Some people are scripted as hypersexual, and others sexually cold and uninterested. People of all genders are taught to be opposing opposites, yet somehow expected to work together if each will just fall into an outlined pattern somehow "designed" for success.

This kind of advice gives the impression that we are no deeper, nor our relationships deeper, than mere behavioral conditioning. We've received the message that our true relationship happiness lies in attitude and rigid role-following rather than true connection and the true discovery of intimacy. We're told that to be happy, we must change who we are and fit into someone else's concept of what we should be. If we listen to contemporary theory, we ultimately believe our relationship success lies in listening to varied outside sources, rather than knowing the abilities and instincts God has placed within us to live and seek intimate relationships.

Our ability to be intimate as human beings proves to us that we are capable of more than operating by surface instructions and basal instincts. We are both designed and equipped to function intimately with other people. How do we do this? We first identify ways to dig beyond the superficial realm of relationship interaction so we can find something much deeper.

What is intimacy?

Solomon's Song of Songs.
(1:1)

(Related Bible references: Ruth 1:16-17, 1 Samuel 18:3-4, 1 John 4:8, 1 John 4:18)

If we properly understand the Song of Solomon to be about something deeper than the surface, we can find evidence of it in the first verse. "Song of Songs" is superlative. This means that it is the most excellent of songs, something high and exalted, and something praiseworthy. There is a unique excellence contained in this book – something that is beyond that which we can find in this earthly realm. Its contents express an attribute and a relationship characteristic that is more than just a physical – or natural – element. It is a heavenly song, something sung in both this world and the next, expressing a longing for something more, deeper, more profound, more powerful, and more intimate than can be achieved in the earthly realm alone.

What is this 'thing' that is beyond earth and the earth realm? It is something people long for and desire. Some discover it in their lifetimes, and others do not. Some find it in a marriage, some in a friend, some in deep community connections, some found it in the "one that got away," and all are purposed to truly find this within their relationship with God. This superlative quality, something beyond all others, is intimacy.

"Intimacy" is a big word with a lot of contexts. Intimacy has been defined throughout the ages in many ways and by many people. The term is used in a variety of ways, from a euphemism for sex to describing intimate communication. When speaking of intimacy that can exist between people, sex and intimate communication can both be extensions of intimacy, but true intimacy cannot be defined by sex and suggestive communication. People can have sex without intimacy and communicate without intimacy as well, which means using these two facets as the crux of intimacy is incorrect.

So, what is intimacy? I define intimacy as knowing by the Spirit. It is being so deeply aware of a person and who they are that knowledge of them exists impossible without such. In knowing someone by the Spirit, words are not necessary some of the time. It is love beyond words. Intimacy is knowing someone beyond description, beyond reason, beyond this realm into the picture of divine love. In that knowledge, a person doesn't have to constantly explain themselves to the other person. The two share something: they share a knowing of the other that others do not have of them. In that knowledge there is a comfort, a trust, an unbreakable bond that withstands anything because that knowledge sustains the storms, the weathering, the hurts, and the difficulties. It is the deepest possible love that can exist: it is a truly beautiful thing, the drive and search for oneness. Oneness does not mean the two become the same, fail to lose who they are, or fail to lose their own identities. It is not dependence; it is a choice two people make as they rest in the knowledge that comes from knowing by the Spirit. Sex often comes because of intimate relationship because, in these instances, it is the most powerful form of communication that can come. When all the words have been spoken and the relationship revels in the unspoken, sex becomes a physical means of oneness, perfect and pure in its purpose, power, and pleasure.

In this world, I believe intimacy is something most people seek but seldom find. In mistaking intimacy for sex, marriage has become the vehicle for sex rather than intimacy. While the Song of Solomon does speak of sex (and very graphically, at that), it does so because sex can be an expression of intimacy. It reminds us of the need for love, in its varied forms, to be demonstrative. It is also a very visual picture of the concept of intimacy in people's lives. We need to be careful, however, to make sure that we do not understand all sex as an intimate expression. Just like all relationships are not intimate, neither are all sexual dynamics. If we study the Bible carefully, we see sex has occurred all throughout history between people in all sorts of circumstances: prostitution, unmarried partners, procreative purposes, rape, incest, adultery, marriage, and beyond. As perhaps the world's most powerful driving force, sex has been used for all sorts of means throughout history. The pagans recognized the powerful force present in sex to the point of incorporating it into their worship and rites without recognizing intimacy in those rites. Throughout history, sex has been used as a means of control, a physical drive, and to satisfy several different needs a person may have. Today we recognize sex, we recognize relationships, and we even recognize concepts about marriage; but we still do not recognize intimacy.

We need to be clear to also recognize that intimacy is a dynamic between people that may manifest in several ways. While sex is often a part of intimacy, it does not have to be. Our understanding of intimacy needs to transcend beyond just physical expression. Ruth and Naomi are an example of a powerful and intimate dynamic existing between two people of the same sex (Ruth 1:16-17). We do not have evidence they were physical lovers, but they shared an intimate and special bond, a knowing and understanding between one another. David and Jonathan are another example of two people with an intimate bond that was not sexual in nature (1 Samuel 18:3-4). Some modern leaders and scholars alike attempt to make the relationships between Ruth and Naomi and David and Jonathan sexual – when we have no such indication – because they are overlooking the underlying dynamic of intimacy that existed between them. Ruth saw Naomi as a mother figure, as a friend, as one with a shared experience (they both lived through incredible loss), as a woman who was struggling, and as one with a promise to fulfill – not as a lover. David and Jonathan likewise saw the bond of battle, friendship, shared experience, and lifelong camaraderie. When we see intimacy in this way, it is an essential dynamic that reflects God's divine love – His *agape* love – between people. Just as God loves us because it is Who He is (1 John 4:8, 1 John 4:18) rather than who we are, this intimate bond of love transcends in the same way. In intimacy, His love becomes a part of us, and a part of who we are. It is what it is, and it is either there, or it is not. We can't force intimacy, nor can we fabricate it, because it is God's hand of connection reaching out through and between two people. The Song of Solomon speaks of the lovers not just as lovers, but as friends – and a chorus or company of "friends" are also included in the recitation, thus sharing in the participation of intimacy – which affirms, yet again, that intimacy is far more than just sex or a physical dynamic. When we stop attributing intimacy to a mere sexual connotation, we will come to see its greater purpose in our lives and its benefit for us as believers walking with God and one another.

The attribution of this song, either written by or for

Solomon, makes this dramatic recitation more than just an arbitrary poem. We've already recognized it as the ultimate of songs, but it has another value as well. The fact that this writing is either attributed to Solomon by writing or was written for him makes it a royal song. This writing expressed something more than common: it was fit for a king, worthy of recitation and presentation in the royal courts.

As we understand the earthly things to be a type of heavenly things, if this song was fit for the king of Israel, it is certainly fit for our Heavenly King, and its attribution and authorship is fit for Him above. We need to pay close attention to this facet of the Song of Solomon because very few books are specifically identified as being of royal note. The relationship dynamic presented here – that of intimacy – is more than just any old, ordinary relationship. Every person alive today knows that anyone can get married if they are of legal age and obtain the proper paperwork. Anyone can think someone is attractive and hop into bed with them. There is something special in here, something divine; something heavenly; and something royal that is to be noted. Intimacy is heaven-sent, it is superlative, it is ultimate, and it is royal.

Even though the world we live in is superficial, I believe most people in this world desire more than a life lived on the surface. We have a longing for connection, love, and a profound sense of meaning and belonging in life. Intimacy and intimate connection with God and one another are how we achieve this in our lives. The search begins and ends with intimacy. Finding it, and maintaining it, however, is often a challenge.

Searching for intimacy

All night long on my bed
I looked for the one my heart loves;
I looked for him but did not find him.
I will get up now and go about the city,

through its streets and squares;
I will search for the one my heart loves.
So I looked for him but did not find him.
The watchmen found me
as they made their rounds in the city.
"Have you seen the one my heart loves?"
Scarcely had I passed them
when I found the one my heart loves.
I held him and would not let him go
till I had brought him to my mother's house,
to the room of the one who conceived me.
Daughters of Jerusalem, I charge you
by the gazelles and by the does of the field:
Do not arouse or awaken love
until it so desires.
(3:1-5)

I am sure that you, as the reader, are curious as to the shift in focus that has occurred. We went from the first verse of chapter 1, which sets the stage for the intimacy of the book, all the way to chapter 3, which has a very different tone. When reading the Song of Solomon chronologically, this shift is particularly notable. Chapters 1 and 2 give a playful, intimate banter to searching for the absence of a lover. Why would this shift be made in this book?

If we desire more than the superficial in a world that we admit is superficial, we need to realize that intimacy comes with its challenges. The first battle is to find someone that we can be truly intimate with. Intimacy is not something that we find in every relationship we will ever be in, nor is it something that we find very often. As something to be cherished, intimacy is not something to take lightly – it does not come along very often.

How do we discover intimacy? As the text indicates, it is something people often look for, in any variety of places. Many search their lives over, settling for relationships that are less than ideal, only to give up on the principle that intimacy exists. In my own life, I came to believe I was incapable of intimacy, and lived in that way, searching aimlessly for something that I couldn't even identify. I have come to discover this is far from uncommon. Love and intimacy are unconditional principles. No matter how jaded we may perceive ourselves to be, a there is a part of us that seeks genuine connection with someone else. Desiring connection, people look for any means they find of it, and try to hold on to that which is only an illusion of it. This is because, as human beings, there is more than one way we can connect with others – and it is possible to mistake another means of connection with intimacy if we do not understand what makes intimacy different from other forms of connection.

In this life, we can connect with people in three possible ways. We can connect to people in a carnal, or earthly way; in a soulish, or emotional way; and in a spiritual way. The carnal, or earthly level of connection, is not what you may think it is. We have come to define "carnal" as sexual, but that is not how I am using it here. A carnal knowledge of someone is simply knowing them as they are in this world, and for nothing more; there is no real relationship there. It is vague knowledge of another fleshly being walking around on this planet. An emotional connection is when a relationship exists between people with a certain level of knowledge of that individual. It is beyond the surface, or casual level, and goes into developing a like or bond with that person. A spiritual knowledge of someone is to know them by a connection that is beyond emotions and beyond something describable in the natural world.

Intimacy falls into the category of a spiritual connection. Even though the partners feel certain things toward each other, intimacy is beyond mere feelings. It is something that has a way of just being. It's not something carnal, merely emotional, or distantly spiritual. It brings reality and insight to the immediate on a spiritual level that is practical in approach and powerful in reality.

The best way I can describe discovering intimacy is to

follow the advice of the Scriptures: do not arouse, nor awaken love until it so desires. Throughout life, we will be infatuated, attracted to, and interested in multiple people. Very few people experience only one attraction throughout their entire lives; most experience different levels of interest and connection with others throughout life. Many may look good to us, but the reality is that intimacy is about more than infatuation, attraction, and personal interest. Discovering intimacy is different. Just like the woman mentioned in the above verses, we can search for more, hope for more, want more in different people and in different avenues – and not find it. Intimacy finds us. We can search for it, we can look for it, we can even try to produce it; but in the end, intimacy finds us. It is self-subsisting, a force of life all its own. When we know it's there and the relationship is safe, we fall into it. We can have been in dozens of previous relationships, but somehow...intimacy is different.

It's hard to explain in words what makes intimacy different. On the surface, the man and woman in the Song of Solomon seem to go on and on about all the same things other people do: they talk about physical attributes, physical desires, and a longing for each other. Poets, musicians, artists, and authors have spent millennia trying to explain just what makes intimacy different. The major difference between intimacy and other relationships is the Spirit. When a couple is truly intimate, there is something between them that is not so much what is spoken, but what remains unspoken. The same is true of those who have tried to give description of intimacy throughout the ages. Intimacy can be defined in words, but it is an abstract which must be experienced. The Song of Solomon is a book to be experienced; it is something to be lived, pursued, felt. It cannot be understood through mere exegesis or hermeneutics. It is love in action, intimacy in dynamic, and an eternal ultimate song that we too can sing...as intimacy finds us.

Battling for intimacy

Beloved

I slept but my heart was awake.
Listen! My lover is knocking:
"Open to me, my sister, my darling,
my dove, my flawless one.
My head is drenched with dew,
my hair with the dampness of the night."
I have taken off my robe—
must I put it on again?
I have washed my feet—
must I soil them again?
My lover thrust his hand through the latch-opening;
my heart began to pound for him.
I arose to open for my lover,
and my hands dripped with myrrh,
my fingers with flowing myrrh,
on the handles of the lock.
I opened for my lover,
but my lover had left; he was gone.
My heart sank at his departure.
I looked for him but did not find him.
I called him but he did not answer.
(5:2-6)

(Related Bible references: Amos 3:3, 2 Corinthians 6:13-15, Matthew 6:24, Malachi 2:16, Isaiah 61:3)

One of the things that many believe about intimacy is that it creates a fairy-tale reality, a relationship free of problems and difficulties. Such romantic notions are far from the truth about intimate relationships. Fairy-tale realities are not intimacy; they are escapism. It is true that truly intimate partners often find ways to work out their differences and often come together in a deeper way because of them. This does not mean, however, that intimate relationships are without the human elements of conflict or difficulty.

Intimate relationships often go through phases. Just because we discover an intimate relationship does not mean it will not change, deepen, or yes, even experience conflict at some time. In the beginning, relationships are generally governed by a playful intimacy. As a couple gets to know one another, the general light-hearted tone keeps intimate companions curious, excited, and delighted. This ensures the intimate partners will become more intimate and knowing of one another. This exciting phase is an acknowledgement and acquaintance phase.

As a relationship grows, the dynamics of intimacy begin to change. When a couple has knowledge of one another, they start to focus on other things about their partner and other things in life. This shift in focus is not negative; it is a maturing of the relationship. Relationships should fit into the larger picture of life rather than being someone's life. As this focus shifts, couples often go through transitions. The transitional phases found as couples shift in discovery of their own levels of intimacy may be difficult, rocky, rough, and intense.

It is a mistake to think intimate relationships are without issues. Intimate relationships still consist of people, and people have issues. Throughout the Song of Solomon, we hear references to the various insecurities, hurts, and wounds the couple bears as human beings. All intimate relationships go through difficult periods, ones in which the struggle for intimacy seems like a battle. It does not mean all hope is lost if a couple is going through an intimate battle. There is a difference between a lost relationship or an irreparable one and one that is having some challenges. The difference lies in the couple's connection: if the couple's intimacy is lost or found not to exist, separation often becomes inevitable. If intimacy remains but seems challenged or changing, it is just a battleground period.

The world is full of challenges to intimacy, both

natural and spiritual. As sin rules in this world, the sinful nature of human beings seeks to divide and conquer rather than unite and celebrate. History is full of stories of unrequited love, people separated by families or death, war and its toll on relationships, bitter feuds, divorce, and separation. In the spiritual realm, we find people martyred, killed, or persecuted as they struggle to maintain their intimate relationship with God. As a result, intimacy has become a struggle, a battle to maintain in a world intrinsically hostile toward it.

Intimacy is not all fun and games, but it is something worth fighting for. Intimacy is something lived through life. It is living deeper than we may in an average relationship, where we can only expose the parts of ourselves we deem worthy of exposure. A deep part of intimacy is the healing that comes about within the individual because they find someone they cannot hide from. When in intimacy, the other individual knows everything about us, even without speaking the deeper hurts we may experience as people. There will be things that come up, in the general course of life, that we do not expect and that deeply hurt us as individuals. As with any relationship, temptations exist to flee from or create barriers as isolation is sought. Every person in a truly intimate relationship has the choice to stick out difficulties, especially personal hurts and wounds, while relying on the one they love to help them through it.

When issues come up, the survival of intimacy in a relationship reaches a point for which it must be fought. If we look carefully, there are two main conflicts between the couple in the book: one in chapter 3, and the other in chapter 5. It is obvious that, as the couple in the Song of Solomon continue their relationship, they are progressing through stages of intimacy – and are now ready to fight to maintain what they have.

One of the most notable things about the conflict in chapter 5 is the way the woman seems to be deliberately avoiding intimacy. Her beloved comes to her in the night, and she thinks of reasons why she does not desire to go and meet with him. She would have to put on her robe, her slippers, get out of bed, go to the door, and meet him. It sounds like so much work – so much of a chore! By the time she gets up to greet him, he is gone, and she must look for him. Her avoidance of intimacy soon turns to regret when she realizes what she has lost.

This is not nearly as uncommon as we might like to think it is. Whether it is out of fear that someone may really know us, we do not want to get so close to someone else, or we have things that prevent us from being comfortable with intimacy, there are lots of reasons people may find to avoid intimacy or deliberately seek to destroy the intimacy present in their relationships.

How do you know when to fight or when to move on? That is the question of the ages, and it does not have many easy answers. The determination goes to those in the relationship, but it can generally help in discerning the situation at hand and see if there are major signs present that intimacy is beyond restoration. In understanding intimacy as a dynamic, we also must understand barriers and blockers to intimacy. In keeping with the precepts discussed here – the search for something deeper – the barriers to intimacy are things that create superficial relationships. These three are alienation, adultery, and abuse. When these three are present, either individually or in combination, they can cause a severe upheaval in an intimate relationship. They can also be signs that a relationship is not intimate by nature and does not have the capability to be such. All these different barriers are both causes and symptoms in many cases, but they tend to be big signposts to an erosion of intimacy in a relationship.

- **Alienation:** Alienation is another term for isolating oneself, but it has a different connotation. Alienation indicates isolating oneself from another person for some reason. There can be any number of reasons why someone may alienate themselves from another person – and some of those reasons may be justified, and some may be unjustified. The symptoms of alienation are any type of avoidance of another in any conceivable way: physical (touch), emotional (discussion, personal sharing, feelings), mental (refusal to share thoughts or ideas, harbors bad thoughts about an individual), or sexual (refusal to engage in any sort of sexual activity unless such is not a part of said dynamic). When someone is in an alienated state, they are unwilling to engage in any intimate involvement or communication with another person. The longer alienation persists, the deeper it grows and the worse it can become. Alienation can be a very difficult barrier to overcome, especially given the reason or reasons for alienation. If it is symptomatic of a relationship problem, alienation is that much more difficult to replace with intimacy. If alienation exists for an extended period, it is often safe to say that intimacy will not return.

In both chapters 3 and 5 of the Song of Solomon, the couple was clearly apart, but not alienated. The woman experienced the temptation to alienate herself from her loved one but overcame this temptation and persisted to try and find him, once again. There was an upheaval that resulted from them being apart, and the emerging battle was to find a place of intimacy (being together) rather than separation (being apart). There is a big difference from periods of separation that may result over the natural course of a relationship and being alienated from one another. As they were apart, the woman sought her lover – she sought to be with him, realizing the solution to restore a sounder sense of intimacy in their relationship was to be together. Alienation sees the solution as a state of separation.

People can be alienated from one another and living in the same house. Couples who are alienated from one another are not always divorced. The state can exist and persist for years, until one of them dies or leaves the situation. Most marital situations I've seen involve some level of alienation, especially if one or both parties in a couple do not believe in divorce. They think staying matters, even if a couple is not rightly together in a marital sense. What many fail to understand is a permanent state of alienation is akin to divorce, without legal jurisdiction.

If we are to examine the principle of alienation from a spiritual perspective, alienation represents a sinful state – it represents the opposite of intimacy. It does not indicate the couple is somehow sinning in the sense of personal sin, but it is analogous to the condition of a human being before they are able to come into a relationship with the Father through Christ. They are alienated – unable to bridge the gap – to reach a point of intimacy once again. It is a place where a relationship has reached a state of hopelessness and irreconcilability. The longer a couple stays in a state of alienation, the more impossible reconciliation becomes.

- **Adultery:** Many people talk about adultery exclusively in the context of sex with someone who is not their legal spouse. I believe the definition of adultery needs to be broader and yet more defined than that. In Old Testament times, God spoke of Israel's idolatry as being comparable to adultery. This means that natural adultery illustrates a spiritual principle. We should pay careful attention to both the natural and spiritual to gain a better understanding of God's illustration present therein.

If we understand adultery and idolatry to stand

spiritually equivalent, then the natural realm understanding of adultery is placing anything in an intimate relationship that does not belong there. The definition of an intimate relationship, however, does not fall into the category of a legal document. People can be together for any number of reasons, and none of those reasons be built upon true intimacy. The result of such a placement is alienation, as one chases after something foreign and the other is left feeling abandoned. By this measure, adultery can take any number of forms. A person can commit adultery with another person physically, but there is also the realm of the "emotional affair," by which someone grows emotionally involved with someone other than their intimate partner in a dynamically intimate way. Affairs often start in intimate ways: conversations that seem "supportive," attention to one's personal likes and dislikes, and affection or attention showered on a married partner that they don't find with their spouse. One can also have an "affair" with their ambition, career or employment, entertainment means, own sense of self or adoration, or any other thing that comes in an intimate relationship in a way it should not.

This does not mean people should not have friends, or that friendships, jobs, entertainment, or other things should be treated with suspicion. An intimate partner can become an idol if they are not understanding of the true trust and flexibility present in intimacy. Intimacy does not mean a person loses themselves or must forsake relationships, friendships, and interests to be in that relationship. What it does mean is certain levels of intimacy are reserved exclusively for that intimate relationship. Recognizing this principle helps guard privacy in intimate relationships and protect them from invading outside forces.

The teachings on adultery in the Scriptures also make it very vital we attend to our spiritual unions as well as our physical ones. The best precaution we can take against adultery is to ensure the right environment for a long-term intimate relationship will exist. This is a preliminary measure that can save a lot of headaches, heartaches, and difficulties later, as relationship dynamics begin to change and complicate through the years. Yes, people do change at times, and yes, sometimes people have alternate sides to them that do not come out early enough to make a decision based upon them. However, there are also instances where we do not listen to spiritual instincts and enter into an unequal yoke because we are pursuing a relationship for a wrong reason.

The Scriptures advise us that two can only walk together if they are agreed (Amos 3:3). In 2 Corinthians 6:13-15, the Apostle Paul speaks against the mixing of spiritual systems in worship. While sometimes used as an attack on interfaith marriage, I believe the advice Paul gives us serves a different purpose in an intimate relationship. The advice herein is practically spiritual; it relates to our spiritual lives in a practical way. In this passage, the Apostle Paul used a common agricultural imagery to teach a spiritual principle. Oxen were yoked together using a yoke (something used to bring two oxen together so they could work together) for plowing and farming purposes. If one ox was smaller than the other, stronger than the other, or older than the other, the yoke would be uneven. In this state, it was impossible for the oxen to work together. While people try to argue the intent of the passage, the Word is showing forth the reality that people cannot work together if they do not agree on a spiritual and practical level.

There are many ways people can be unequally yoked. It's not all about which church you go to or everything that you might believe (especially those things that are different). It is important to see an unequal yoke as a barrier to intimacy. It is not as simple as defining an unequal yoke by what church someone attends or someone's doctrinal pursuits. You can live with a person who goes to the same church as you and who seems to have the same belief system, but discover they have an entirely different perspective that creates a barrier. People can be unequally yoked due to economic, educational, cultural, emotional, political, and spiritual perspectives. The basic principle of an unequal yoke is an inability to walk together in agreement on an important foundational matter. Unequal yokes are about more than just differences of opinion. No two people on this planet agree about every single issue in existence. An unequal yoke happens when a couple tries to maintain two radical differences based on life foundations.

Adultery comes into the picture because two are not agreed. This parallels the Biblical comparison to adultery and idolatry: they are both disagreeable systems. Thus, adultery is a symptom of this irreconcilable disagreement. It represents a lack of choice. The Scriptures teach us we cannot serve two masters (Matthew 6:24); and adultery is attempting to satisfy the needs of the spirit-man or woman without doing what is necessary to truly bring about that satisfaction. If a relationship is to an adulterous point, the relationship is not a relationship any longer. Rather than trying to straddle two fences, such a situation must be dealt with, and decisions must be made. Such decisions guard both personal intimacy and spiritual well-being.

Given this understanding of adultery, it is very easy to see how people enter adulterous affairs and relationships: their own relationship lacks something either conceptually, intellectually, physically, sexually, or spiritually, and they try to find it in someone else. It is the same principle as those who find something lacking in an area of their lives and try to fill that void with an idol.

It is also important to see that adultery dictates us to take preventative measures before entering a long-term commitment with a partner. The presence of intimacy must be there for a relationship to work in the long run. Anything but intimacy sends us wandering and looking for something beyond what we can find in that relationship.

- **Abuse:** The Bible states that violence breaks the covenant (Malachi 2:16). What covenant is the Bible speaking about? Yes, it is obvious the immediate context of the passage speaks of the covenant that exists between God and human beings. The violence spoken of in the passage, however, is violence between domestic partners – thus, it also refers to the covenant arrangement relating to intimacy that exists in relationships.

  Abuse is best described as a violent disruption in a relationship designed for intimacy. In addition to any physical or mental damage done, the violation of intimacy in an abusive situation always takes a spiritual toll on an individual. In many instances, the individual may not even be able to explain exactly how the abuse has affected them as a person; they simply know it has. The violent disruption of abuse may take many forms: it may be physical, sexual, emotional, spiritual, or mental. Depending on the severity of the experience, a person may take many years to heal from abuse. One of the long-term side effects from abuse is difficulty maintaining intimate relationships with other people.

Abuse is a particular threat to intimacy because it can disrupt it long after the perpetrator is gone from someone's life. It can affect one's ability to withstand intimate relationships in the future, and miscommunications with others in intimate relationships, because others do not understand the reasons why intimacy is difficult for the abused individual.

The deep and difficult wounds of abuse only heal by deep love. An individual who has been intimately abused needs to experience the love of God in a way that transforms their ashes into beauty (Isaiah 61:3). This comes about through time; there is no quick fix. Those who are in an abused person's life need to demonstrate true love while upholding boundaries that edify and empower love in someone's life. Giving somebody their way all the time or giving in constantly because one feels bad for someone who has been abused is not good for them. Upholding and emphasizing love both for one's partner and oneself shows forth what true love is. It echoes how God loves us: He extends Himself to us in the ultimate way, while upholding boundaries and limits that establish what is good for us in the long-term. The abused individual needs to see love as an unselfish power, something that is about the good of everyone rather than the love of self.

Because violence breaks the covenant, abuse as is present within a relationship that is supposed to be intimate, but is not, is particularly damaging. Abuse in any form can cause such a strain, intimacy is either non-existent or unable to form. The constant disruptions can cause the relationship dynamics to quickly spiral out of control.

Alienation, abuse, and adultery are all a part of this present world. In an ideal setting, they would not exist. Understanding that they are here means they may be a part of any relationship, no matter how it may look or seem to be from the outside. Intimacy demands we are more than surface deep. Just because a couple has been together for an extended period does not mean they are not battling barriers to intimacy.

When people are battling with intimacy, they require support and non-judgment. If someone decides a relationship dynamic is so unhealthy it needs to end, that decision should be supported. If someone feels they need to walk away from something because it is hurting them, that decision should be supported. The church should be doing what it can to preserve and foster healthy relationships rather than encouraging couples to stay in damaging or destructive situations. It should not be about the number of couples who stay together just to stay together, but the number of healthy relationships fostered and encouraged by the Kingdom environment found therein. Intimate battles are not won through blind or legalistic attitudes but come about through true Kingdom love and principle. Not all relationships last, but all relationships will battle. How the battle ends depends on much more than someone's willingness to stay together: it also depends on the level of intimacy present, and the dynamics present in intimacy. The sooner we understand this, the sooner we can begin helping people rather than upholding institutionalism.

Identifying intimacy

Come with me from Lebanon, my bride,
come with me from Lebanon.

Descend from the crest of Amana,
from the top of Senir,
the summit of Hermon, from the lions' dens
and the mountain haunts of the leopards.
You have stolen my heart, my sister, my bride;
you have stolen my heart
with one glance of your eyes,
with one jewel of your necklace.
How delightful is your love, my sister, my bride!
How much more pleasing is your love than wine,
and the fragrance of your perfume than any spice!
(4:8-10)

So, if the Bible depicts intimacy as so wonderful, even with its battles and complications, how come it isn't easy to identify? How come there isn't some big neon sign hanging over the man or woman that we can be intimate with? Why do we have to waste time testing out various relationships?

There are a lot of reasons why dating can be very beneficial socially, and we will discuss these reasons in the next chapter. On a practical level, meeting many people and "testing the waters," so to speak, helps us to identify better what we seek in an intimate partner. It also exposes us to a variety of intimate relationships. Not every person we discover a level of intimacy with will become a long-term relationship for us. Some people are better suited as intimate friends, some are people worthy of our trust, and some people are just there for a time, while others stay for awhile or always. The level of intimacy we achieve with our first love when we are in our early teens is totally different than the intimacy we seek when we get older and can enter long-term life relationships. Being able to interact intimately helps prepare us throughout our lives for different levels of intimacy with people and helps us to be intimate people, both sincere and profound.

How people discover intimacy in their own lives is often unique to the individual at hand and the way God interacts with them, and they with one another. There are a couple of key things, though, that people often report with intimacy – and I can vouch for them myself, as well:

- **"Love at first sight":** In the passage above, the man says of the woman: *"You have stolen my heart, my sister, my bride; you have stolen my heart with one glance of your eyes..."* In other words, it was a case of what we might call "love at first sight." Some people say they believe in love at first sight, and others do not. Most people (myself included) said they didn't believe in it...until it happened to them. Love at first sight isn't what is often depicted by the media. It's not this instant moment where you want to jump into bed with someone else or find someone so lustfully attractive, you can't control it. It doesn't necessarily happen the second two people first meet. Love at first sight is a moment of connection by which a divine spark ignites between two people. There is just something there, something unexplainable, that the two can identify is there, but can't make sense of it to other people. In intimacy, this establishes that the potential for the relationship to grow into more than a fly-by-night experience. It establishes the principle for long-term connection.

A side note: love at first sight is the idea that there's something special between you and someone else, but it doesn't always mean long-term intimate relationships happen immediately. "Love at first sight" is that "aha moment," that moment when you know something special is present herein. It's not always something you experience right away. Sometimes that "aha moment" is found in long-term friendships, it arises after you date someone a few times, or maybe something you realize in someone you've known after you've known them awhile. It's not always instantaneous, but is just as important, regardless of when it happens.

- **Your partner sees you as a person:** People tend to objectify their partner when relationships lack intimacy. If you are seeing your partner as someone to help cover the bills or as someone to sleep with until you get bored, your relationship is objectified. In true intimacy, your relationship is based on a unique vision: they see you as a person, and you see them as a person. Neither of you is a strange extension of the other, nor does one try to change the other. There is a mutual respect, as well as a mutual love.

- **You don't have to try to get their attention; you have it:** This is an interesting facet to intimacy because it is the opposite of what we have been told to do for so long. From the time both boys and girls are young, we are hearing how to dress to be noticed, whether it is for being cute (as a child) to getting attention from someone (as a teen and later an adult). The message society gives us is clear: you have to try and get someone else's attention – and such is accomplished through a certain style of dress, physical characteristics, or behaviors. In intimacy, you find the opposite. You don't have to do all the things you always did – you have your partner's attention. The man and woman in the Song of Solomon take attention to an interesting level: it's almost as if no one else in the world exists. This is how intimacy is. You are aware there are other people, but they are of no threat, nor distraction to you and your beloved. Gone are the days where you feel that a tight pair of jeans or a great pair of pantyhose will turn someone's head. In intimacy, someone's head has been turned, but not because of those things. It has turned simply because they love you.

A side note: Having someone's attention doesn't mean they don't have other things in their life that also demands attention. Nobody can be everyone's focus all the time. We still must focus on things such as God, work, household chores and responsibilities, family obligations, and general life. This doesn't mean you don't have your partner's attention…only that life requires us to pay attention to many things. As much as any one of us might love to focus on our partner exclusively all the time, we know that, in being grown, responsibility means couples work together rather than pouting when necessary things arise that demand time and attention.

- **It's not about what anyone else thinks:** When we live in the world, we operate our relationships by the world. How many of us tried to date the popular boy, girl, trans, or non-binary individual, just to be seen with them? We are fooling ourselves if we think we outgrow that mentality when we graduate high school. If anything, relationships can easily continue to be a means by which we climb the social ladder and "be seen" with the right people. This is because relationships are often used incorrectly as a social entity rather than the building block of intimate connection. When someone is in a truly intimate relationship, it isn't based in what anyone else thinks. It is not about who likes who you are with, how being with that person can change your social status, or how you feel the two of you look together. It's not about anyone except the connection you have with that person, and the rest simply does not matter.

- **The relationship is not based in expectation:** Traditional relationships revolve around expectations to be met. Both people come into a relationship expecting the other person to do certain things or meet with certain requirements that create the foundation of the relationship. In intimacy, however, there are no expectations. The relationship provides a sense of comfort and companionship, and you just want to be with someone to be with them. It's not about doing so much as about being.

- **You feel like you are still yourself, yet there is something different about you:** This is the hardest aspect of intimacy for me to describe. When in intimate relationships, we discover a greater sense of ourselves. This is because intimacy is a place of ultimate honesty, not achieved in any other setting. It's a real place, where the real you can come out. So much of our life interactions take the form of dishonest courtesy with others – but not so in intimacy. In intimacy, we find ourselves and are a truer sense of ourselves. At the same time, this place of honesty creates something new within us; something different, something more profound. We don't really become a totally new person, just a person we didn't know we could become.

- **A sense of respect is present:** You can tell when a couple respects one another: they aren't threatened by each other. Too many relationships today are competitive to the core, with intimate partners trying to outdo each other. Intimacy does not need to compete because an appreciation exists, one to another, in acceptance.

The most profound relationship anyone can have – either in this life or in the next – is one born and based in intimacy. Intimacy teaches us about ourselves, about one another, and about our relationship with God. In the next chapter, we will be looking at the dynamic of intimacy, especially how that dynamic changes our perception of relationships all together.

CHAPTER 2

Women and Men (and Everyone Else)

Key verses

- **Verses 1:5-6:** *Dark am I, yet lovely, O daughters of Jerusalem, dark like the tents of Kedar, like the tent curtains of Solomon. Do not stare at me because I am dark, because I am darkened by the sun. My mother's sons were angry with me and made me take care of the vineyards; my own vineyard I have neglected.*

- **Verse 2:4:** *"He has taken me to the banquet hall, and his banner over me is love."*

- **Verse 2:7:** *"Daughters of Jerusalem, I charge you by the gazelles and by the does of the field: do not arouse or awaken love until it so desires."*

- **Verse 2:15:** *"Catch for us the foxes, the little foxes that ruin the vineyards, our vineyards that are in bloom."*

- **Verse 3:5:** *Daughters of Jerusalem, I charge you by the gazelles and by the does of the field: Do not arouse or awaken love until it so desires.*

- **Verse 3:11:** *Come out, you daughters of Zion, and look at King Solomon wearing the crown, the crown with which his mother crowned him on the day of his wedding, the day his heart rejoiced.*

- **Verses 5:7-8:** *The watchmen found me as they made their rounds in the city. They beat me, they bruised me; they took away my cloak, those watchmen of the walls! O daughters of Jerusalem, I charge you-- if you find my lover, what will you tell him? Tell him I am faint with love.*

- **Verse 6:1:** *Where has your lover gone, most beautiful of women? Which way did your lover turn, that we may look for him with you?*

- **Verse 6:9:** *But my dove, my perfect one, is unique, the only daughter of her mother, the favorite of the one who bore her. The maidens saw her and called her blessed; the queens and concubines praised her.*

- **Verses 8:10-12:** *I am a wall, and my breasts are like towers. Thus I have become in his eyes like one bringing contentment. Solomon had a vineyard in Baal Hamon; he let out his vineyard to tenants. Each was to bring for its fruit a thousand shekels of silver. But my own vineyard is mine to give; the thousand shekels are for you, O Solomon, and two hundred are for those who tend its fruit.*

Words and phrases to know

- **King:** From the Hebrew word *melek* which means "king."[1]

- **Chambers:** From the Hebrew word *cheder* which means "chamber, room, parlor, innermost or inward part, within."[2]

- **Adore:** From the Hebrew word *'ahab* which means "to love; to like."[3]

- **Dark:** From the Hebrew word *shachor* which means "black."[4]

- **Lovely:** From the Hebrew word *na'veh* which means "comely, beautiful, seemly."[5]

- **Veiled women:** From the Hebrew word *'atah* which means "to cover, enwrap, wrap oneself, envelop oneself; to grasp."[6]

- **Handsome:** From the Hebrew word *yapheh* which means "fair, beautiful, handsome."[7]

- **Rose of Sharon:** From two Hebrew words: *chabatstseleth* which means "meadow-saffron, crocus, rose"[8] and *Sharown* which means "plain, level; the district lying between the mountains of central Palestine and the Mediterranean Sea and north of Joppa; a district on the east of the Jordan around Gilead and Bashan."[9]

- **Lily of the Valleys:** From two Hebrew words: *shuwshan* or *showshan* which means "lily"[10] and *'emeq* which means "valley, vale, lowland, open country."[11]

- **Lily among thorns:** From two Hebrew words: *shuwshan* or *showshan* which means "lily"[12] and *kho'akh* which means "thorn, brier, bramble, thornbush, thicket; hook, ring, or fetter."[13]

- **Beloved:** From the Hebrew word *dowd* meaning "to love; by implication, a love-token, lover, friend; specifically, an uncle: (well-) beloved, father's brother, love, uncle."[14]

- **Sons:** From the Hebrew word *bane* meaning "a son (as a builder of the family name), in the widest sense (of literal and figurative relationship, including grandson, subject, nation, quality or condition, etc."[15]

- **Little foxes:** From two Hebrew words: *qatan* or *qaton* which means "young, small, insignificant, unimportant"[16] and *shuw'al* or *shu'al* which means "fox, burrower."[17]

- **Ruin the vineyards:** From two Hebrew words: *chabal* which means "to bind; to take a pledge, lay to pledge; to destroy, spoil, deal corruptly, offend; to bring forth, travail"[18] and *kerem* which means "vineyard."[19]

- **Daughters of Jerusalem:** From two Hebrew words: *bath* which means "daughter; young women, women as a personification; daughter villages; description of character,"[20] and *Yeruwshalaim* which means "Jerusalem = teaching of peace; the chief city of Palestine and the capital of the united kingdom and the nation of Judah after the split."[21]

- **Desert:** From the Hebrew word *midbar* which means "wilderness; mouth."[22]

- **Daughters of Zion:** From two Hebrew words: *bath* which means "daughter; young women, women as a personification; daughter villages; description of character"[23] and *Tsiyown* which means "Zion =

parched place; another name for Jerusalem especially in the prophetic books."[24]

- **Faint with love:** From two Hebrew words: *chalah* which means "to be or become weak, be or become sick, be or become diseased, be or become grieved, be or become sorry"[25] and *'ahabah* which means "love; God's love to His people."[26]

- **Perfect one:** From the Hebrew word *tam* which means "perfect, complete."[27]

- **Blessed:** From the Hebrew word *'ashar* which means "to go straight, walk, go on, advance, make progress."[28]

Comedian George Carlin once summed up relationships between men and women like this: "Here's all you have to know about men and women: women are crazy, men are stupid. Women are crazy because men are stupid."[29] We laugh at this because we identify with it. In our crazy world, the interactions between men and women seem divided along strict lines that cause both confusion and upheaval. If you listen to conventional sources, they tell us men and women will never understand each other. Men find women complicated and daunting, and women find men simple and clumsy. We've been described as being from totally different planets, totally different mindsets, totally different diets, and controlled by totally different hormones. The world gives us the message that men and women will never bridge the gap and can never bridge the gap. Even the church upholds double standards, teaching that men and women are so different, they can't even function within the same spheres of life. Are they right? Is there any truth to this?

Then, as we delve into modern society, we see the

advance of non-traditional relationships, such as those between partners of the same sex, outside of the gender binaries, or who don't fall into the categories of traditional norms. While we are more familiar with traditional images, many queer relationships often suffer from similar awkwardness, disconnection, and issues that we see in more traditional relationships. How do we bridge relationship gaps across the board?

The bridge between the binary sexes (while the text does speak of men and women specifically, this doesn't mean other genders are excluded) lies in intimacy. Solving the gap between "crazy and stupid" doesn't lie in self-help books, it lies in coming back to a place of true love and companionship with one another. If we look back at Adam and Eve, the first sin divided them from one another (Genesis 3:8-19). This change in dynamics makes other people seem alien to one another and impossible to figure out. If we look at the Song of Solomon, the couple doesn't seem so different; they seem complimentary. Whatever their differences or self-conscious issues may be, they do not seem to be that much of an issue for them.

If we truly believe the genders across the spectrum are meant to exist together (as most of do) then that means intimacy is not only a possibility, but also a requirement for successful relationships. In intimacy, we see that men and women, binary and non-binary do have differences, but in many ways, we are not all that different. As human beings, we all seek to be loved, accepted, purposeful, and seen for who we really are. We all need to be with someone who uplifts and holds us, keeping us in an honest and secure place. We all need to reach out to our Creator and find a purpose in that. When we look at things like this, our ability to communicate as men and women, as binary and non-binary, grows more possible and more powerful...as it is done by the Spirit.

Knowing who you are

Beloved

I am a rose of Sharon,
a lily of the valleys.

Lover

Like a lily among thorns
is my darling among the maidens.
(2:1-2)

(Related Bible references: Genesis 1:27-28, Genesis 2:18-25, Esther 2:1, Esther 2:3, Esther 2:12, Psalm 45:11, 1 Peter 3:3-4, 1 Kings 22:5, 2 Chronicles 18:4, Matthew 6:33, Romans 12:1, Galatians 2:20)

The Song of Solomon operates by a progressive revelation of intimacy. Each chapter, verse, and thought continues in the next, or somehow reiterates an earlier principle. At times, the concepts overlap or pick up again at another point in time – but continue the progressive revelation of intimacy contained therein. The result is a beautiful flow of thoughts, each one as important as the other. In this progressive revelation, we learn much about intimacy, but also much about the principle of progress in God. All throughout history, God has worked by progress. Everything done by God, in God, and for God comes about by His divine timing and process. So many things in the spiritual realm come about by process: creation, birth, transformation, sanctification, healing, and yes, intimacy. As intimacy stands as a repairer of humanity's breach one to another, intimacy is too a process. The Song of Solomon shows the progress of intimacy: from interest to consummation, and everything in between. It also delicately reveals the conflicts, results, and issues. The Song of Solomon is anything but unrealistic; on the contrary, the complications of this discovery and its conflicts are powerfully played out.

The initial conflict is shown to be within, especially here in chapter 2. The fact that the beloved declares about herself first, and her darling second, shows us the order to intimate understanding. As we know ourselves, we are better able to know others. We cannot enter true intimacy without an awareness of ourselves. Intimacy is not the absence of self; it is the complement of it. Rather than understanding relationships as the emptying of self, it's important we see those we become intimate with as a compliment. Adam and Eve did not cease to be themselves in the garden; they simply became a compliment to one another (Genesis 1:27-28, Genesis 2:18-25). In the wake of the fall, the complementary nature of man and woman became antagonistic. Thus began the eternal struggle between men and women for control, whereby attributes are now used against men and women in their relationships. Suddenly, men and women are expected to "change" for each other. Queer individuals are supposed to somehow be "other" than they are. Is this a divine idea? Certainly not! Intimacy never asks someone to become something other than who they are and who God has created them to be. If being with someone causes a person doubt, self-dislike, or damage (even on an emotional level), the relationship is abusive. Such plays up the antagonism between men and women and re-emphasizes isolation, rather than intimacy.

These verses of the Song of Solomon affirm the essential component of individual self within a relationship. Getting caught up in endless romantic dynamics does not create true intimacy, nor does it lead to happiness in long-term relationships. If we don't understand who we are, a relationship will not help us delve into intimate understanding. Instead, we will find ourselves lost in a seemingly unending struggle, forever seeking a purpose and identity in someone who cannot help us get to our true selves.

The beloved begins with a statement of identity: she

compares herself to the rose of Sharon, and a lily of the valleys. She knows who she is, she knows how special and unique she is, and she knows what she carries with her. By modern standards, this comparison sounds vain, if not odd. Few women today would be willing to compare themselves to flowers, no matter how rare or uncommon. Why is such a comparison relevant?

The rose of Sharon is a term used to refer to many different species of flowers found throughout the world. Many theories surround what plant it refers to in the Song of Solomon: it could be a reference to a type of lily, tulip, shrub plant, or the crocus plant used to grow saffron. All these references establish the rose of Sharon as unique, yet common enough to recognize. The rose of Sharon plant is not so obscure that it cannot be identified, but also not so common that it loses its specialness. Both the rose of Sharon and lily of the valley are known by scent, color, and unique shapes. They are prized, purposed, and honored for their beauty, scent, and esteem.

In the midst of desert conditions, these beautiful flowers were a welcome sight to ancient peoples. They signified life, health, and hope. So too, this woman recognized herself to signify these things. Amidst the millions of women in the world, she was unique and special, prized to offer something that another woman could not. She was a beacon of life, health, hope, and truth. Her beauty was noted, as who she was stood out from among the crowd. In a world full of people who blend in, she radiated something deeper and more appealing than the rest.

In modern society, we prize conformity and denounce uniqueness. The beautiful roses of Sharon and lilies of the valley are criticized, condemned, and told to hide their uniqueness in favor of looking like everyone else. Too many denominations force women to dress according to certain rules, forego caring for themselves, and display an outer neglect that reflects the inner snuffing of their shining light. Women must be encouraged to be themselves; be unique, beautiful, and shining, however they are called to do so. They should be encouraged to make the outside reflect what is inside, through proper care (Esther 2:1, Esther 2:3, Esther 2:12, Psalm 45:11, 1 Peter 3:3-4). God has given each one of us unique qualities by which we are able to bless the world. These unique qualities must be fully embraced, both by the woman and her intimate partner. Each woman must feel confident enough to proclaim herself unique and beautiful, fully understanding the anointing and gifts God has placed within her. Anything less is a deterrent to intimacy.

Within Christianity, we have come to note Jesus as the Rose of Sharon and the Lily of the Valleys. Many find this odd, especially given the one speaking in the book is female. The connection to the believer is obvious: Jesus is rare, life, hope, and light in a world of conformity and dry desert. She recognizes Him within her, working and being the source of her inner beauty and strength. Her connection is to her first love, her Lord, in all things. It is truly our understanding of ourselves as God reveals that brings forth our inner beauty. It is only when we understand who we are in Him and what we bring that we can be intimate with another. If we will only set the Lord first, the rest will follow (1 Kings 22:5, 2 Chronicles 18:4, Matthew 6:33).

The Scriptures have affirmed these things specifically for women for a reason: because the world always seeks to create women in the image of male purpose and desire. The church is as guilty of this as the world, echoing worldly concepts and ideals about women. This is an echoing of the antagonism present between the sexes due to sin. These ideas distract from the beauty and gifts given to a woman by her Creator, thus rendering intimacy difficult for a woman uncertain in herself. In today's church, women seek to affirm themselves through their mates. It is their hope that an intimate partner will tell them who they are, and they will come to discover it from that. This passage of the Song of Solomon clarifies such thinking is wrong. Women must know who they are to have that mirrored or affirmed by an intimate partner. The lover himself affirms her uniqueness and beauty in verse 2: he knows what he's got. He knows how special she is, and how blessed he is to have her. Out of all the women in the world, he has a woman who knows her Lord is living within her (Romans 12:1, Galatians 2:20) and has bestowed a powerful purpose for her life. She is not an extension of him, but of the One Who created her, saved her, and redeemed her. To her lover, she is a gift; to be cherished, to be valued, and to experience a unity with, unlike that shared with any other on this earth.

<u>Becoming most beautiful</u>

Beloved

How right they are to adore you!

Dark am I, yet lovely,
O daughters of Jerusalem,
dark like the tents of Kedar,
like the tent curtains of Solomon.
Do not stare at me because I am dark,
because I am darkened by the sun.
My mother's sons were angry with me
and made me take care of the vineyards;
my own vineyard I have neglected.
Tell me, you whom I love, where you graze your flock
and where you rest your sheep at midday.
Why should I be like a veiled woman
beside the flocks of your friends?

Friends

If you do not know, most beautiful of women,
follow the tracks of the sheep

and graze your young goats
by the tents of the shepherds.
(1:4-8)

Friends

Where has your lover gone,
most beautiful of women?
Which way did your lover turn,
that we may look for him with you?
(6:1)

Lover

You are as beautiful as Tirzah, my darling,
as lovely as Jerusalem,
as majestic as troops with banners.
Turn your eyes from me;
they overwhelm me.
Your hair is like a flock of goats
descending from Gilead.
Your teeth are like a flock of sheep
coming up from the washing.
Each has its twin,
not one of them is missing.
Your temples behind your veil
are like the halves of a pomegranate.
Sixty queens there may be,
and eighty concubines,
and virgins beyond number;
but my dove, my perfect one, is unique,
the only daughter of her mother,
the favorite of the one who bore her.
The young women saw her and called her blessed;
the queens and concubines praised her.
(6:4-9)

How beautiful your sandaled feet,

O prince's daughter!
Your graceful legs are like jewels,
the work of a craftsman's hands.
Your navel is a rounded goblet
that never lacks blended wine.
Your waist is a mound of wheat
encircled by lilies.
Your breasts are like two fawns,
twins of a gazelle.
Your neck is like an ivory tower.
Your eyes are the pools of Heshbon
by the gate of Bath Rabbim.
Your nose is like the tower of Lebanon
looking toward Damascus.
Your head crowns you like Mount Carmel.
Your hair is like royal tapestry;
the king is held captive by its tresses.
How beautiful you are and how pleasing,
O love, with your delights!
Your stature is like that of the palm,
and your breasts like clusters of fruit.
I said, "I will climb the palm tree;
I will take hold of its fruit."
May your breasts be like the clusters of the vine,
the fragrance of your breath like apples,
and your mouth like the best wine.
May the wine go straight to my lover,
flowing gently over lips and teeth.
(7:1-9)

(Related Bible references: 1 Peter 1:22, 1 Corinthians 11:1-16, Hebrews 9:26-28, 1 John 2:2, 1 John 4:10, 1 Peter 3:2-5, 1 Corinthians 6:19, 2 Corinthians 4:7, Genesis 1:26-27)

What defines beauty? The pursuit of what is beautiful has been both challenged and examined throughout the arts for ages. If there is one historical fact about beauty, it is that it changes from era to era. In intimacy, however, whatever society deems as beautiful is often inapplicable. Being in a deep, intimate relationship is beautiful all by itself – but it also makes us beautiful. Having someone in our life, who loves us unconditionally and sees us beyond imperfections and flaws, changes how we feel about ourselves, and how we perceive the changes that we go through in our lives.

The Song of Solomon spends an extensive number of verses (as can be seen by the passages above) devoted to descriptive words as the lovers describe the depth of their attraction to one another. Their descriptions, to some, may seem over-the-top. Nobody talks like that, right?! Be that as it may, the truth is that when people love one another in an intimate bond, what they share is something that manifests in a true appreciation for one another physically as well as in other ways.

The physical interests in the Song of Solomon go far beyond appreciation of standard body parts deemed attractive today. The examination and celebration of a diversity of body parts: legs, breasts, feet, navel, waist, neck, eyes, nose, head, hair, height, temples, teeth, and mouth offer credibility to the fact that appreciation of form and beauty takes many different forms. There's not just one thing or a couple of things that might draw or attract someone to someone else. Celebrating different physical attributes is part of body positivity. The Song of Solomon reminds us that body positivity is part of intimacy, and is something to both be celebrated and acknowledged.

If we were to look at the man or woman for ourselves, odds are good that we would probably not find them nearly as attractive as they found each other. Looking at the man and the woman through their eyes is almost impossible. Why? Because we cannot see the depths of what they saw in one another. Attractiveness is something measured by far more than physical attributes; it is also about loving someone for who they are. Even though we may not see the couple as they see one another, this kind of true appreciation is something we can see and have in our own intimate experiences. When we know someone on such an intimate level, a true beauty is revealed to us that we see in them physically, emotionally, and spiritually.

Nowadays people spend millions of dollars annually to obtain tanned and darkened skin. Today, people consider this a sign of beauty – something noteworthy and attractive. Biblical people would have found our modern obsession with obtaining suntanned skin an absurdity. In ancient times, lily-white or light skin was prized. The reason for this was not rooted in primitive racism (as it was observed within all cultures, even among those with dark skin), but in class distinction. Darker skin – tanned or burned skin – was an indication that someone worked in hard labor. Lighter skin was a sign of privilege, not having to work out in the fields as a laborer or slave.

With this understanding of the terminology used in verse chapter 1 verse 5, why is such a statement made here: *"I am dark, but lovely?"* The woman proceeds to explain why she has such dark skin – not just addressing her lover, but also the daughters of Jerusalem and her friends. In the case of a lover, and especially of an intimate companion, and anyone else, for that matter, why is such explanation necessary?

The woman is speaking eloquently and defensively at the same time. She is not explaining herself, but her situation, because the results of such are obvious for others to see. She has a "wounding," something in her life that is clearly there for others to see. Her skin has been darkened as the result of a deep wound by those who knew her intimately in her life. The passage speaks of her "mother's sons," or her half-brothers, who, having control over her in her life, forced her to do their hard labor. The Scriptures only tell us they were angry with her. It doesn't say why they were angry or what they were angry about, only that they were angry with her, so they forced her to do their share of the work. Her dowry, or inheritance for marriage, was left to ruin because of how she was treated. Her dark skin is a reminder of her state of labor, of financial poverty, and of intimate wounding.

As we prepare to enter an intimate relationship on a new level, we are often aware that we have "dark skin." Every one of us has been wounded by an intimate companion, whether it was a relative, friend, boyfriend or girlfriend, lover, or ex-husband or ex-wife. There is something about us in our lives that stands out due to a generated hurt or offense. Intimate pain is that which hurts us as a person. There are many who spend their entire lives looking for ways to heal such hurts. Intimate wounds are something we regard as unappealing or unlovable within ourselves. We can begin, over time, to define ourselves by our dark skin – by that very thing which wounded our identity so long or so recent ago.

There is something powerful in this relationship dynamic, however. The woman recognizes that even though she is dark, she is lovely. Through her hurt and her wound, she recognizes herself as beautiful. Some might say that she is beautiful despite her intimate pain, but a true believer in the Lord recognizes her as beautiful because of what she has been through. There is something to be said for enduring and surviving the worst of pains, the worst mistreatment, and coming through to the other side. In that comes beauty, a profound beauty that cannot be taken away due to age or inflicted evil. The intimacy present in her relationship with the beloved helps her to see herself differently. Wrong relationships (those that cause intimate violation) cause us to see ourselves as damaged, bad, wrong, and even useless. They re-emphasize things we already perceive to be wrong with us, even if they are not really as serious as we see them. Right relationships (those that edify intimately) help us to see ourselves as beautiful. Studies have shown the importance of this principle in intimate relationships for both women and men.

The powerful principle of love covering a multitude of sins (1 Peter 1:22) is at play here. Love doesn't just cover the sins that a person commits themselves. True love –

intimate love – can also help heal and cover those committed against that person. The deep wounds of life are only healed by deep love. This means that intimacy holds within it a true dynamic reflecting God's love of hope and healing. Those who are intimate with others need to avoid re-opening and re-emphasizing old wounds. Whatever the "dark skin" may be in someone's life, a proper and truly loving intimate partner will not deliberately seek to hurt the other person with that wound. Deliberately using what has already intimately wounded someone to wound them again is, in common vernacular, classified as "hitting below the belt." True intimacy does not violate the other person, but covers them by love, and tends to that wound with love; anointing it and soothing it, showing forth true beauty can come from even the most painful hurts.

Before God, we are too "dark, but lovely." All our lives we deal with the dark stains of sin and the hurts and pains of life. When we come before God, we are wounded. As we walk with God, He transforms our ashes into true beauty (Isaiah 61:3). God's love covers our sins and those committed against us. Through our relationship with Him, He transforms us, restores us, and loves us. True intimacy with God is a healing power all its own, because God is our true Healer, Restorer, and the first Love of our lives.

The imagery of the woman in terms of wound and shame continues in verse 1:8, where she speaks of being among 'veiled women.' In Old Testament times, prostitutes veiled themselves as to avoid identification in public. We can see these different traditions changing, as in the New Testament regions infiltrated by Greek culture, the practice was for all women to veil themselves as a sign of modesty (1 Corinthians 11:1-16). We can gather from her terminology two things: the first is the association of shame and of shaming oneself. The second is the reason of such: because if she disguised herself as such, she could spend more time with her beloved.

We are moved by this incredible expression of love: the

woman was willing to disguise herself among the prostitutes to have a chance to be with the man she loved. This kind of gesture, often interpreted as love, is more appropriately deemed as desire. The beloved and lover desired more time together. Culture demanded members of the opposite sex could not show any gesture or affection in public. As was custom, they were not even allowed to speak to one another. The amount of time the two would have had together would have been greatly limited.

Most adults in modern society have difficulty understanding this concept, because social intercourse is largely unregulated among adults across modern cultures. The picture of men and women in Middle Eastern and many Muslim countries worldwide can give us an idea of the restrictions on men and women in public. As most reading this probably never lived in the Middle East, it's beneficial to remember something we can identify with. Remember back, if you can, to the days of early dating when you were in junior high or high school. At that young age, there was obvious need for supervision – and most of us got just that. We only saw our first love or early love during specified periods of time, and it was never enough for us. School, home, not being able to drive, and not being able to see one another as we might have liked was regarded as an inconvenience. At that point, we would have done anything to be with our significant other: sneaking out of the house, lying about our whereabouts, skipping classes, even hiding out in the hallway on the way to one class or another. It didn't matter if what we did raised eyebrows from adults or earned us a reputation – we believed our partner to be worth it. The same is a parallel to the desire to be together that the woman sought with the man in her life here in the Song of Solomon. Extended periods apart made the heart grow fonder, and the longing to be together more intense.

She was willing to get a reputation, people to discover her wounded nature, or even be caught in a dangerous spot to be with her beloved. How do we feel about those around us? Are we willing to sacrifice to be with the other person? Sometimes we are in situations where the littlest compromise, sacrifice, or call to give something up sends us into a rage. We may be unwilling to compromise in any way for the other person in the relationship. We need to examine ourselves in such a situation. What is the root of such an unwillingness to bend? Is it selfishness? Fear? Is there unresolved anger? Bitterness? Unforgiveness? Or is it something more? Is God speaking to us in our circumstance and telling us this person is not right for us? Is the relationship not benefiting the Kingdom – let alone the people in the relationship? Does something not feel right? When we are in a relationship with someone – no matter the type of relationship – the desire to be together should exist. If that desire, that willingness to give up one thing to be with someone isn't there, it's time to find out why. It's not always the flesh or selfishness talking, especially the more we press in and the more resistance we find within ourselves. Sometimes it is that we are attempting to force an idol upon ourselves, a foreign god, as God screams out to us in our circumstances to avoid the road we are forging without Him.

The reason how we perceive our relationships and our willingness to give of ourselves even through sacrifice to another is because this parallels our relationship with God. God has given all to us through the Word made flesh, His Son, Jesus Christ (Hebrews 9:26-28, 1 John 2:2, 1 John 4:10). That ultimate sacrifice has been made to overcome the powers of death and sin. In turn, we should be willing to sacrifice and give our all to be with God and in the presence of God. Nothing that God asks us should be too great for us to do. None of us has the right to deny the requests of God. We should be willing to make any sacrifice required to maintain our relationship with Him, even if that sacrifice means the death of our physical being or some part of our flesh that stubbornly holds on. Just as Esther was willing to make the ultimate sacrifice, first being in the harem and then breaking the law to go before the king, we too need to be willing to sacrifice ourselves to be with God at all costs. As nothing can separate us from the love of God in Christ (Romans 8:37-39), we should not allow ourselves to be separated from God in any way, shape, or form.

What does it mean to be the "most beautiful?" As the Song of Solomon is already a book expressing the superlative, it is no wonder that it speaks in superlatives: in the case of this passage, of being "most beautiful among women." This same sentiment is echoed multiple times in different chapters, as can be seen above. Our culture spends millions of dollars per year on exterior beauty. From cosmetics to various cosmetic procedures, the pursuit of beauty is a big business industry. There is nothing wrong, according to God's principles, in accentuating one's features and practicing the physical hygiene that leads to beauty. We should want to accentuate the beauty God has given us for His glory and as a testament to Him. Nobody likes to look at something haggard, old, unkempt, dirty, and unattractive. God has created us to be attractive and beautiful, one to another. This comes as we focus on and develop the beauty that comes from within (1 Peter 3:2-5). It does not mean we neglect our outward appearance, but that we attend to that which is within. To be "most beautiful" comprises three different components: caring inward, caring outward, and caring about what one does and who one is around. These three components make up the "most beautiful" because they enhance and allow for intimacy to flow within our lives:

- **Caring inward:** We need to attend to our inward being. This means that we are people of God's Word who operate by God's Spirit and are empowered by the Holy Spirit. We must attend to our spiritual being and ensure we have spiritual well-being operating and flowing within us. Walking with God in our lives and getting ourselves right with Him is where intimacy can begin to flourish in a deeper way within us. As we apply God's precepts to our life and walk deeply with Him, we can develop inner beauty.

- **Caring outward:** The Bible tells us we are the 'temples of the Holy Spirit' (1 Corinthians 6:19). While some teach that we should neglect our physical bodies, this is not what God's Word teaches us. God has given us a treasure in these earthen vessels, our bodies (2 Corinthians 4:7): and that treasure is His Spirit working within us. The excellency that is of Him (2 Corinthians 4:7) needs to shine through what He has given us. If the body is created in His image (Genesis 1:26-27), we need to care for the body through hygiene, good care, exercise, diet, and physical well-being. Physical, emotional, and mental hindrances block our ability for intimacy – so caring for our bodies enables us to be able to walk in intimacy with God and others in our lives.

- **Caring about what one does and who one is around:** If we don't like who we are around or what we are doing, it hampers our physical, emotional, psychological, and spiritual well-being. It also hampers our interest or pursuit of intimacy. The Song of Solomon tells us that if you wanted to find the most beautiful of women, she could be found with her beloved! Just follow the flocks and the herds to where he was! We will be most content when we are where God – our true Beloved – would have us to be. We are most beautiful when we are in His will and doing what He would have us do! Every other love in our life will line up with this, and we will have an equation to be most beautiful!

Men, women, and marriage

Beloved

How handsome you are, my lover!
Oh, how charming!
And our bed is verdant.

Lover

The beams of our house are cedars;
our rafters are firs.
(1:16-17)

(Related Bible references: Ruth 3:1-18, Genesis 24:1-67, Matthew 1:18-19, John 4:16-18, Ephesians 5:22-33, 1 Peter 3:1-7, Psalm 1:3, Jeremiah 17:8)

The man and woman in the Song of Solomon give us a very private glimpse into a world that few dare to go: their most intimate lives. The home and family are oft discussed in the church but are not discussed in terms of intimacy. The reason for this is simple: the family is viewed as an institution rather than as a unit of intimacy. It is treated as an assembly-line production with a desired result, ignoring the purpose and beauty of intimacy that can be created therein.

Marriage throughout every age has served more political and social needs than emotional, physical, and spiritual. Marriage and family serve as a slogan for politicians, a selling point for media products, and an agency to preserve finances and bloodlines. The familial relationship, as a building block of society, has served to provide alliances, financial restitutions, security, and status all throughout history. If we look at history from its true realism, marriage has been used and abused rather than truly edified. We are deluding ourselves if we believe marriage goes without abuse today. Even though arranged marriage is not an active part of western life (arranged marriage is still prevalent in some Asian nations, and many western couples face pressures to marry certain individuals of particular status to this day), marriage itself remains under its greatest threat and assault as it is exploited and used to serve an agenda rather than glorify God.

The Song of Solomon proves that true marriage – a marriage built upon a foundation of love and intimacy that God has put together instead of man putting it together – can't be reduced to roles and politics. Politics and agendas were never intended to be a part of home life. The underlying purposes of marriage and family life were to extend intimacy toward one another and allow those building blocks of intimate relationships to benefit and solidify God's Kingdom.

One of the ways marriage has been most misused is in the way it has been used to oppress women. Instead of edifying women in intimate relationships, marriage has been used as a vehicle to abuse, imprison, and damage women. In making marriage a vehicle for patriarchy, abuse and mistreatment naturally follows. Most relationship pitfalls are blamed on women, no matter what true circumstances may exist. Women are expected to be at the beck and call of men, changeable to their whims, and at their very service. Many believe men have the right to treat a woman however he pleases. Such attitudes have caused women to be oppressed in the most intimate of ways, and subject to the vilest treatment. Women are regarded as purposed to procreate and meet the sexual interests of men, void of enjoyment and forced to participate against both will and virtue.

It's unfortunate to realize that, while we may view arranged marriage or child brides as archaic, we do not view the mistreatment of women as such. The church has been one of the worst perpetrators of female oppression within marriage due to misinterpretation of the Bible. The biggest mistake we make is that we interpret the entire

Bible according to two or three Bible verses about relationships rather than interpreting two or three passages about relationships according to the entire Bible.

The Bible does not support a subordinate position for women in relationships. There isn't a typical 'pattern' of courtship or dating. In the book of Ruth, Ruth is the one who approaches Boaz about a marriage relationship (Ruth 3:1-18). Isaac's marriage arrangement with Rebekah (Genesis 24:1-67) was far different than Mary's arranged marriage to Joseph when she was most likely between 12 and 14 years of age (Matthew 1:18-19). The Samaritan woman at the well was not condemned by Jesus for living with a man to whom she was not married (John 4:16-18). The woman in the Song of Solomon is as much a pursuer of the man as the man is of her. She expresses physical, sexual, and practical interest in her lover. He desires to love her and be with her, caring for her and supporting her – and her equally with him. There is an intimate flow of equality that moves between the two in a perfect balance and harmony. It isn't about who dominates the other, but about allowing each partner to be exactly who God has created them to be.

The "submission" teachings found in Ephesians 5:22-33 and in 1 Peter 3:1-7 exist to establish the important understanding that Jesus Christ is the head of everything, including the home and intimate relationships. This is a statement of sovereignty designed to prevent against evils, abuses, and an improper sense of lordship within the home. In ancient Roman societies, male householders had legal permission to do just about anything they desired, which meant they needed a reminder that they, too were accountable to God. Men need to know they are not the head of the household, nor is the woman – but Christ is truly the head of it all. Wives are not encouraged to relate to their husbands in a special way, but in the same way that all believers are encouraged to submit one to another. This means that a wife is to interact with her husband in a practical sense as she would any other man. She is not to make him an idol, nor is she supposed to ignore him or treat him with disrespect. She is not expected to be treated in any way other than that which is godly and upholds God's precepts for righteous conduct. Husbands are to love their wives, dealing with them unselfishly, considering their needs, and making sacrifices for them, as necessary. The Bible addresses specific areas of note between men and women in the marital relationship, but it also does something else: it encourages balance between the two. The reason for this is simple, and echoes back to our initial point: marriage is a type, and a reality. Marriage isn't designed to be about vows, politics, and bondage: it's also a type of Christ's relationship and with the church. Keeping this in mind reminds us that in intimacy, there is no violence, nor dominance; only respect, love, anticipation, and excitement.

As part of intimacy between human beings, we find the verdant bed. To be "verdant" means to be lush, green, and healthy. It is the will of the couple that they may have an active and healthy sex life. They did not view sex as shameful but looked forward to it with purpose and excitement. This is not about a procreative symbol, but about an intimate power. The New Testament tells us the marriage bed is undefiled (Hebrews 13:4). This means when it comes to relationship intimacy, sex is an indicator of the health in that relationship, unless there is some reason why a sexual relationship is physically impossible. If a couple has issues with sex, there are most likely other issues that are manifesting through the sexual relationship. Even though it's often the first place a couple will notice, sexual issues are often the last place where marital discord shows up. There are many reasons for this, and one of the most obvious is because sex is often such a taboo subject, even within a relationship. Relationship issues manifest through sex because it is an easy target to manifest issues.

Relationships are complicated. Partners bring their baggage from life and past relationships into their current situations. When it comes to sex, we also bring social mores and religious concepts. If the marriage bed is undefiled, the only way it becomes verdant and healthy is through communication. Communication is an essential aspect to intimacy. When communication waivers or grows nonexistent, sex becomes a more distant aspect of a relationship because sex is, in and of itself, a form of communication. It is a physical relation between men and women that says everything ranging from "I find you attractive" to "I love you." Sex can also give a message that is unsafe, one that speaks violation (such as sexual abuse or rape). It's important couples talk about their feelings, attitudes and beliefs about sex, because this is how a healthy sexual relationship develops. Neither the man nor the woman should ever feel demeaned sexually by their partner, because such an attitude erodes at the intimacy between the two.

The verdant bed also echoes a place of safety. The marital bed is about more than just sex; it is about a safety in physical intimacy. Couples should feel comfortable discussing and expressing matters pertaining to sex to one another. There aren't any "shoulds" or "should not's" in intimate sex. The dynamics of the relationship and the specifics of those dynamics are unique to the couple, and something private between the two of them. The only thing that is definitively off limits is sexual activity that goes against the will of the other party, thus violating the safety contained therein. We know that violence breaks the covenant (Malachi 2:16) and sexual violence breaks the covenant of intimacy God designed for such a relationship.

Talk of the bed moves to talk of the home, as the two are often a natural progression. Intimacy between a man and a woman can lead to children, which leads to the expansion in a family. Speaking of the house built with cedars indicates it is built with strength and fortitude, not easily broken down and not easily succumbing to attack. Households built upon the Lord, based in intimacy, based in mutual love and respect for one another are those that survive the storms of life. Couples should discuss their beliefs about family and having children prior to marriage, along with their discussions about sex and sexual matters. Intimacy cannot be achieved without truth, and the intimacy that exists within a family varies between the members. The intimacy between a parent and a child is different than the intimacy that exists between a husband and a wife. It is different because intimacy extends; it grows and develops, ever-widening and never decreasing. Just as the firs of Lebanon shield and protect from storms, displaying flexibility and stability, so too the intimacy of the family should help train up its members – whether husband and wife, parents and children, siblings, or extended family – in the various ways to weather the storms of life. Intimacy makes life livable, enjoyable, and meaningful. Paralleling our relationship with God, it too makes our life livable, enjoyable, and meaningful, but it also does something else: it makes it purposeful. We learn how to weather the storms and difficulties of life as we stand in the righteousness and learning of the Lord. Just like the tree planted by the waters, our essential communication with God helps us develop the necessary righteous character to remain unmoved by life's storms (Psalm 1:3, Jeremiah 17:8). Staying rooted in the family of God as well, the Body of Christ, His Church, keeps us focused, purposed, and ready for all that is to come.

Overcoming sexism

Daughters of Jerusalem, I charge you
by the gazelles and by the does of the field:
Do not arouse or awaken love

until it so desires.
(3:5)

(Related Bible references: Amos 3:3)

One of the most unique aspects about the Song of Solomon is its attention to women – and the forward and forthcoming nature displayed by the women in the book. The women in the Song of Solomon are anything but passive or resisting. The third chapter of the Song of Solomon goes on to charge the daughters of Jerusalem. Why are they specifically addressed in this way? As we have already seen, everything in the Song of Solomon has a meaning. According to the Hebrew, the term "daughters of Jerusalem" can have many varied meanings, including:

- Daughters of Jerusalem (the literal city)
- Young women of Jerusalem (the literal city)
- A personified woman, signifying God's people, such as the church of Jerusalem (found in the literal city or associated with the church in the literal city)
- The sub-cities of Jerusalem or of the larger group of God's people
- The daughters of peace
- The people of God (church) of peace
- The churches of peace

I believe the Song of Solomon is calling on all the above with a piece of advice. The Scriptures are speaking to God's women, wherever they may be; His daughters of peace; and His people, His churches, wherever they may be in the world. He is speaking to the product of His saving work, His church, through His women, His daughters of peace.

The mention of daughters here upholds and elevates the woman as one charged with a special message, equipped to benefit from the message. We know the woman in the Song of Solomon defies many stereotypes, and her call to specifically address through the language of the daughters compels the further break of stereotypes. The reason these women are addressed echoes the same reason the church is often personified as a woman: because in a woman's very body, she can carry and bring forth life. From the church, personified as a woman, we find the essential message of the life-saving Gospel. It is contrary to God's spiritual flow and His order to suggest a woman cannot carry the Gospel message, for no other reason than the church herself is feminine. The natural order of the woman as life-bearer typifies the spiritual order of the church, and this natural and spiritual connection cannot be rejected, nor denied. Those who reject the woman the right to speak forth the words of life do not rightly understand the role of the church in the Gospel proclamation.

This also raises the relevance of sexism: in the world, in the church, and in the relationship dynamics between men and women. When sexism is present, intimacy cannot be achieved. This is true in an immediate (couples) sense, and a larger (Body of Christ) sense. When one is deemed inferior to another, the two cannot be agreed, and the two, therefore, cannot be one (Amos 3:3). If we study the history of society, we find the most basic inequality among people to be inequality among the sexes, existing long before many other inequalities surfaced.

If a couple is to find intimacy with one another – and the church to find its true intimacy with God – It must put aside its sexism and truly come together, embracing the women of God. Understanding the woman is understanding the church; rejecting the woman is rejecting the church, God's sent-forth source, with the Gospel, in every era until Jesus returns.

The woman's advice to the daughters of Jerusalem repeats her advice in the second chapter: do not arouse or awaken love until it so desires. Given the nature of chapter 3 and its shift in tone, the reason it is reiterated is different. The woman charges the daughters of Jerusalem with her advice again, but in a different context. When it comes to relationships and intimacy, we must be able and ready to deal head-on with the battle. If we aren't ready to fight for intimacy, we aren't ready to be in the relationship.

When it comes to our relationship with God, we need

to be ready to guard the intimacy of the Father in our lives. Life is full of distractions, false gods, and false promises designed to distract us from spiritual things. Many will come and try to draw us away from the love of God, stirring a false love and arousing a false passion that will take us far from where God would have us to be. The words that come to us, as the children of God brought forth from the church, His daughters of Jerusalem, are worth protecting. We need to be willing to fight out that battle against the enemy of God and his minions at every turn in our lives. At the word of God, we go forth; when He calls us to stop, we stop; when He repositions, we reposition. At every careful juncture, we follow His commands for us and with us, in Jesus' Name.

Separate time and creativity

Who is this coming up from the desert
like a column of smoke,
perfumed with myrrh and incense
made from all the spices of the merchant?
Look! It is Solomon's carriage,
escorted by sixty warriors,
the noblest of Israel,
all of them wearing the sword,
all experienced in battle,
each with his sword at his side,
prepared for the terrors of the night.
King Solomon made for himself the carriage;
he made it of wood from Lebanon.
Its posts he made of silver,
its base of gold.
Its seat was upholstered with purple,
its interior lovingly inlaid
by the daughters of Jerusalem.
Come out, you daughters of Zion,
and look at King Solomon wearing the crown,
the crown with which his mother crowned him

on the day of his wedding,
the day his heart rejoiced.
(3:6-11)

(Related Bible references: Job 23:10, Exodus 16:2, Numbers 13:21, Isaiah 33:8, Isaiah 48:21, Jeremiah 2:6, Jeremiah 44:2, Jeremiah 50:12, Lamentations 4:19, Ezekiel 6:14, Ezekiel 29:5, Joel 2:3, Malachi 1:3, Hosea 2:14, Matthew 3:1-3, Hebrews 11:38, Matthew 4:1-13, Mark 1:4, Mark 1:12-13, Luke 1:80, Luke 3:4, Luke 4:1-13, Genesis 1:31, Mark 1:12-13)

Intimacy does not mean we never require personal time or personal space. On the contrary, intimacy allows for partners to spend time with God or on their own from time to time as they develop themselves as people. Intimacy recognizes introspective discovery, and the importance in developing as an individual. The result of introspective discovery leads us to a greater place of intimacy. Sometimes we find what we are looking for; sometimes we find something else entirely; and sometimes we find both what we seek and something extra. The discovery of battle comes forth because we are constantly learning about ourselves, and trial brings out things we did not know were there. As our rough edges are polished, God searches us out, and brings us out shining as gold (Job 23:10).

In the passage above, the woman found her love, which was what she was seeking. She was seeking more than just a person, however. The woman was seeking more than just any man; she sought out the man who stood as an intimate companion. Her search was not just for a man, but for intimacy. In the process, she also found something else: the arrival of the king. In the desert place, one that was dry and dusty, the most beautiful splendor of royalty came forth, bringing royalty with it.

The desert is frequently used in the Bible to illustrate a place of barren nothingness. In contrast with the Promised Land that was said to flow with milk, honey, and the abundance of crops, the desert was a place that flowed with nothing. Time and time again, God's people were brought to the desert when in exile (Exodus 16:2, Numbers 13:21, Isaiah 33:8, Isaiah 48:21, Jeremiah 2:6, Jeremiah 44:2, Jeremiah 50:12, Lamentations 4:19, Ezekiel 6:14, Ezekiel 29:5, Joel 2:3, Malachi 1:3). When God's people were called back to God, they were often called to the desert (Hosea 2:14, Matthew 3:1-3, Hebrews 11:38). Even Jesus spent time in the desert, prior to beginning His three-year ministry (Matthew 4:1-13, Mark 1:12-13, Luke 1:80, Luke 4:1-13).

The reality about desert periods is they often represent periods of trial and discovery – thus, a battle period of sorts – in one's life. The difference with a desert period is it is where an individual or group is left to discern themselves, rather than fight with other people. There's no blame of others in the desert! In the state of nothingness, God can speak, reveal and hear – unlike anything we can receive in the realm of our everyday lives.

In today's church, we hear incessantly about prosperity. Prosperity has become a buzzword to describe greediness. The result is a church left, forever wanting, forever seeking, and persistently dissatisfied. In this never-ending cycle of want, we forget about gratitude. The revelation of God and doing what we need to receive God's revelation is lost in a pandemic maze of things, wants, and unholy desires. This is where the desert comes in. Sometimes we have everything, all except for nothing. The only thing we don't have experience with is nothingness. To find everything, we must find nothing. Out of the desert comes the proclamation of promise and purpose, just as John the Baptist came forth preaching in the desert (Matthew 3:1, Mark 1:4, Luke 3:4). The ultimate promise we seek – the ultimate intimacy – only comes through emptying out our own selfishness and never-ending wants and allowing the Spirit to indwell within us so we can reach out to others. We cannot do this if we are full of personal wants; it can only come about when we reach a desert place within ourselves.

The result that comes forth is a royal splendor, glory,

and true intimacy. From the driest, most barren place comes Solomon, the King of Israel. Here he typifies Christ, coming forth from the desert to begin His ministry. Out of nothing (the desert place) came the King of Kings and Lord of Lords to do the work of the Father. Beauty, power, change, splendor, and yes, even the message of salvation, came up from out of the desert. In nothing, God can and does do something.

To be drawn toward something or someone, we must first put ourselves aside. This does not mean we become floor mats or allow ourselves to be abused, nor does it mean we put aside principles or things that are important to us. What it means is that we must understand what it means to become one beyond trying to conform someone else to our own concepts and ideals. Relationships based on the premise that someone should conform to us are as destructive as those wherein we expect to completely conform to another. Emptying, seeking that desert experience helps us to find much-needed balance our lives need.

I have often taught that in an effort to find balance, we must first find extremes. This serves to find the true middle point, not swaying too far in either direction one way or the other. In a day that is so materialistic, our possessions are interfering in all our relationships, both natural and spiritual. To achieve a state of intimacy, we must reduce ourselves; spend time with God in nothingness, rather than always thinking the key to spiritual prowess and Kingdom vision lies in getting more things.

Solomon arrives not alone, but with an entourage. These warriors were the finest men come forth to do battle, to protect the king in times of defense. Every one of us needs to have this in our lives: we need to have good people who we can rely on for spiritual battle when the time comes. These people represent a special intimacy in our lives, which is why they come up out of the desert with us. These are the people who stick with us, through thick and thin, despite changes and challenges that come our way. As they have become one with God, so we too have become one with Him, and one with them. This special bond transcends the issues that often arise as we go through changes and trials in our lives.

Our friends are part of our intimate lives. We may not often think of such, but it is our friends who get us through the problems with families and relationships, standing through to better days. When relationships fail or hit difficult times, our friends pull us through. When we don't know what to do with our families, it is our friends who give advice, listen, and offer respite. Every one of us should have our own entourage, our community there to bless and encourage as we go through life's ups and downs.

Also relevant in the process of intimacy is creativity. Long ago, people crafted everything they had instead of going to the store and buying mass-produced items. We know from the Word that God, as Creator, brings forth beauty with His creation. One only must look around to see the splendor God has brought forth in power and prestige. God Himself pronounced His creation good (Genesis 1:31). Crafting or operating in another sense of creativity, therefore, unites us to God, as well. Out of nothing, we make something, born of the creativity God has placed within us. In paralleling this, Solomon's ability to craft out his own carriage and make something beautiful out of it echoes God's creative abilities. Within all of us, God has given us the ability to do certain things; to bring forth beauty, productivity, and the product of solid, gifted work.

Walking in the creativity of God is a part of walking in intimacy with Him. Intimacy represents unity, and as we operate in that which He has given to us, it draws us to Him. Working with God in such a way brings us to a greater knowledge of Him. Through such work, we communicate with Him and discover a deeper way in which He is working in our lives.

When in a relationship, the suggestion is made of the importance of doing things together. I think more than just doing things, it is important for a couple to be able to work together in partnership. The reality remains that even couples do not always enjoy the same things, and it is not right to expect someone to constantly do things they don't enjoy doing. Sometimes such a sacrifice is necessary, but couples need to see, uphold, and understand the value in independent interests, activities, and work. The Bible is clear that Solomon made the carriage himself, not Solomon and his wives. They were not expected to stand alongside him, handing him tools as they watched him do something they couldn't care less about. The same is true in reverse. The daughters of Jerusalem came and inlaid the interior, but not until Solomon finished building it. Ancient societies believed greatly in the value of both individual and sex-separated activities for men and women, recognizing that it is important for men and women to work independently, as well as with each other.

Whether we go to the extreme of having sex-separated activities today or our own unique interests, such is both vital and essential to a balanced relationship understanding. Doing things without our spouse isn't the end of the world. If anything, it enhances it. Respect for interests is essential, and encouraging individuality makes things that much more special when it is time to come together again.

The last verse of Chapter 3 starts out with a call to the daughters of Zion. As with the term "daughters of Jerusalem," 'daughters of Zion" can also have a dual meaning. Echoing back to earlier, the call to daughters raises the relevance of God's women. They are called for a special purpose and with a special message. The word "Zion" is often used interchangeably for "Jerusalem" in the prophetic books, but the word "Zion" is totally different in meaning than the word "Jerusalem." While Jerusalem refers to a place of peace, Zion refers to a parched or dry place. The desert mentioned just a few verses up – the desert discussed earlier – is exactly what is called out here. The women of the desert, those in a place of dryness and emptiness, seeking oneness with God and a true sense of intimacy (wherever they may be) are called up and out. They are the first to receive the word – those women who have sought God – that their king has arrived, and to see the splendor therein. Solomon is here, once again, as a type of Christ. This means the women of God, those who know their true union and oneness come from Him, are called forth to meet their King, coming out of their desert place. They are the brides, His brides, which represent the Bride of Christ, coming to the wedding of the Lamb at the end of the age.

If humanity, and especially the church herself would seek God through the process of intimacy, they would find the battle of intimacy to be more approachable and yes, even winnable. In light of this, relationships grounded in true faith and intimacy are less intimidating. To win the battle, we must take proper steps to reign victorious, rather than defeated. Intimacy rules by love, a powerful Biblical virtue connected to God Himself; hurt is overcome by love. If we will only walk deeper in love, we can change the dynamics of intimate battle, for we know that God is love (1 John 4:4).

Relationship security and the little relationship foxes

Lover

*My dove in the clefts of the rock,
in the hiding places on the mountainside,
show me your face,
let me hear your voice;
for your voice is sweet,
and your face is lovely.
Catch for us the foxes,
the little foxes
that ruin the vineyards,*

our vineyards that are in bloom.
(2:14-15)

(Related Bible references: Jeremiah 49:16, Obadiah 1:3, Matthew 16:18-20)

A 'cleft' is a crack or crevice found in a rock. The Bible speaks of people hiding or finding security in a cleft (Jeremiah 49:16, Obadiah 1:3). This echoes the principle of safety and security spoken of earlier in this book, but in a different way. In this particular instance, the woman is hiding in a place of security by herself. She has an anchoring all her own, a security that she finds in the true Rock, Jesus Christ. From this security that holds her grounded and purpose despite what happens, comes forth her true beauty and loveliness. Her lover sees this in her, speaks of her, and is drawn to her for all these qualities. He knows how relevant she is in his life.

The New Testament teaches us that the church is built upon a Rock, which is faith in Christ Jesus (Matthew 16:18-20). It's not an accident the church is spoken of as female, using this same imagery and parallel. The church rises from the strength and security of the rock, to present itself ever lovely and beautiful. When the church or parts of the church attempt to rest herself on rocks other than the true Rock, the church cannot stand triumphant. She is not sought, because she loses her beauty for forsaking her love. If we want to remain beautiful and desirable – both men and women – we must be found in the Rock. If we want the church to remain relevant and purposed – she too must be found in the Rock.

How do people get away from the Rock? How do individuals and relationships reach a point where they fall into a state of disrepair? The answer is found in verse 15, where it talks about the 'little foxes' that spoil the vine. To some, it may seem the poetic lyricism of the Song of Solomon jumped from one topic to an entirely different one, all together. The lover went from talking about his beautiful, beloved woman appearing forth from a rock to talking about catching small foxes that spoil the vineyards. If we carefully see the imagery, we can see he is using a different symbolism to describe the process of destruction. In this highly poetic and lyrical book, we find a powerful principle that applies to every aspect of life: it is the 'little foxes' that spoil the vine.

Today's society focuses a lot on the 'big foxes.' We constantly hear about the big things that hurt people's relationships, as well as the big things that may damage a person's relationship with God, their ministry, or their positioning in the church. We hear about adultery, financial scandals, dishonesty with money, secret relationships gone public, and the consequences of such. The personal decisions affect the personal aspects as well as the professional aspects. These big things, however, don't start out big. Every action people deem major didn't begin with a big action – it started out with something small, something minor, something that wouldn't be considered serious or major to someone else. That little thing turned out to be the foundation of something much bigger and more serious. Every unkind or abusive word, every mistreatment of one's significant other, every time when another was made to feel irrelevant or unimportant – are all "little foxes" that lead to other things.

This verse is here to make us realize little things do matter. They can matter in either direction – either making things better or making them worse. The little bit we feel is not enough can become something big, important, and impacting. Just as seeds start out small and turn into plants that reap a harvest, so we too reap small and sow large. The little things we neglect, do not attend to, or do are the very things that turn into destructive forces. If we want to have good relationships, we must attend to the little things – both positive and negative. This is most evident in our relationship with God. The things we see as small, minor, or unimportant are often some of the biggest lessons, tests, and experiences we will ever have with Him.

The small things lead to bigger opportunities and instances for elevation. If we want to grow in God, we need to pay attention to the 'little foxes.'

Patriarchy and relationships

The watchmen found me
as they made their rounds in the city.
They beat me, they bruised me;
they took away my cloak,
those watchmen of the walls!
O daughters of Jerusalem, I charge you—
if you find my lover,
what will you tell him?
Tell him I am faint with love.
(5:7-8)

Friends

We have a young sister,
and her breasts are not yet grown.
What shall we do for our sister
for the day she is spoken for?
If she is a wall,
we will build towers of silver on her.
If she is a door,
we will enclose her with panels of cedar.

Beloved

I am a wall,
and my breasts are like towers.
Thus I have become in his eyes
like one bringing contentment.
Solomon had a vineyard in Baal Hamon;
he let out his vineyard to tenants.
Each was to bring for its fruit
a thousand shekels of silver.

But my own vineyard is mine to give;
the thousand shekels are for you, O Solomon,
and two hundred are for those who tend its
fruit.
(8:8-12)

It's obvious that the Song of Solomon challenges society's tightly held concepts of relationship roles. We have already looked at this dynamic in the woman herself and the interaction between her and her lover. The forward nature of the woman, of her overly stated desires, her obvious, rather than passive interest, and the man's reception of such without complaint or fuss proves that the concepts we have about men and women are not always Biblical. In fact, the two passages above also challenge roles of men and women in a wider sense: in the sense of patriarchy.

One of the major facets of grace is intimacy, because intimacy reflects grace working in our lives. Even though it is not something we often cognitively understand, it is something that, somehow, some way, by an unexplainable manner, covers and protects us in our lives. It gives us a sense of safety, and the elimination of power and control, which we find dominates in sin. It is God's will that we find intimacy in our own experiences. If we are to find intimacy, we must cast aside the notions that society's relationships governing men and women are the ones God intended for us to have. This means that patriarchy, or the ruling established system by which women are governed by men, must be obliterated. For grace to abound and intimacy to develop, the eternal power struggle created by patriarchy must cease to be an issue in a couple's interaction.

To properly understand patriarchy's impact on women, men, and relationships, we must understand it as a system of oppressive rule. Patriarchy is the belief that men rule the world, but the means by which they rule it relates to household, or small groups. The man is seen in a leadership role, often compared to a father, over that group – and especially over women in that group. When a society believes its men govern its women for no other reason than the men are men and the women are women, the system balance is dangerously unequal. Patriarchy dictates a man is in control of a woman, and this is in a relationship as well as in all situations worldwide. It is the basic message the church gives: that women were created for men and, therefore, are universally subject to men. There is no Bible verse which makes this kind of a statement, and no properly understood Biblical concept which can impose this type of thinking. While it is not Biblical, it is often said to be such because it is extremely cultural. In every major culture worldwide, patriarchy is a dominating facet.

We are deluding ourselves if we believe patriarchy does not impact us today. Despite several waves of the Women's Movement, many relationships still reside in practices and concepts echoing long from the dark ages. What we do not often consider is the level of burden these practices and concepts have upon all of humanity. If a woman makes more money than the man, this is seen as a conflict. If a man wants his wife to stay home and not work, it is still expected she does this, which can also lead to conflict. Society deems certain aspects of both women and men as a joke (PMS, mother-in-law jokes, husband jokes, for example), something to be mocked. The only reason some people marry is to have children, and then experience intense tumult in their relationship choice. Households are considered the ultimate life accomplishment. Those who want more or seek something different are considered selfish, self-centered, or lacking something in their lives.

Then the introduction of the queer community proves even more how deeply patriarchy implodes throughout our culture. The idea that a couple might not require a "man" to "lead" it throws traditionalists into chaos. The fact that some might not only not identify with one of two genders, but neither one, sets the world into a tizzy. Patriarchy tells us things must be one set way, with no allowance for any others. Likewise, it doesn't consider that while most relationships might have followed a specific course, that doesn't mean every relationship in history was always the same way.

Even though we don't think of it in this manner, patriarchal systems lie at the root of these disconnects. We are told that the ultimate life goal for a man is to be the master of a household, with wife and children in tow. A woman's dream is to serve her husband in that household and raise his children. Anything different from or contrary to these notions is regarded with mocking. And, in the process, the rift between men and women gets wider, and communication grows narrower.

Since patriarchy is worldwide, intimacy and relationships are messed up worldwide. Abuses of power result in intimate abuse of women, men may feel more like guardians for women, and women feel as if they are involved with their fathers, and men and women find it difficult, if not impossible, to come to a unified understanding of one another. The consequences of sin reign within relationships, no matter how holy or sanctified people try to be within them.

Patriarchy has hurt intimacy between men and women, women and women, men and men, and between groups of all genders on the spectrum. It makes cultural expectation outweigh the intimate desires of a couple and turned intimacy into a laundry list of rules and regulations. It makes me realize that while some people do fear true intimacy, most people fear the expectations society tries to pass off as intimacy. Somewhere inside of us, our connection to God and one another lets us know society's expectations upon our relationships are harmful to them. We, as people, conditioned to a certain way of doing things, may not always know the way to go, but we do know that something doesn't feel right about the way we have been going.

The Song of Solomon heralds a powerful message to us: We must let intimacy rule our personal relationships, instead of society's regulations, our parent's regulations, and yes, even instead of the advice of well-meaning people. Trying to fix things using worldly methods doesn't fix them; it simply blocks the intimacy we seek to achieve. Intimacy has a way of flowing, all by itself. It takes the sting out of relationship discord and puts it in harmony, a means by which intimate partners can communicate.

Chapter 5, verses 7 and 8 depict the first instance of male domination within the book. The woman, searching for her beloved, finds herself beaten, bruised, and her property stolen by the male guards appointed to watch the city. The text itself indicates she may have been sexually assaulted, as well. The comparison of this today would be a woman out at night, attacked by police. The Scriptures do not give us a reason for the brutal beating, but the ancient culture most likely does. As is the case in many Middle Eastern countries today, being a woman alone out at night is a punishable offense. She stepped out to search for her beloved, and society pounced on her for it. She was punished by a system that, by its arbitrary rules, could have kept her from the one she loves.

History has had a way of punishing forward-thinking and bold women for taking steps in their relationships, especially when the relationship was somehow opposed by others. If we look at what this woman did, she was quite brave in doing it. In pursuit of love, she defied the system. Her love and the safety she found in her intimate relationship pushed her to go beyond the boundaries of what was both acceptable and comfortable.

Love should inspire boldness in women, not passivity. Being in an intimate relationship should inspire women to achieve more instead of feeling like a punishment or a chore. Intimacy is about a connection that creates a safe place where each person in that relationship can become and develop into all they can become. It's not about the stifling of dreams, but about the expansion of them, knowing someone is there to support, no matter what the result is. Intimacy inspires – it is the foundation for creativity and purpose in life.

It's notable that the lovers in the Song of Solomon are not struggling with patriarchal notions in their dynamic. Relationships, marriage, intimacy should not be based on competitive spirits that relate to power, control, and dominance. The lovers cut through the expectations of everyone else and found something beyond the runaround. Even though society might try to control its people, intimacy is something with the ability to go beyond expectation. It's different than dating someone in rebellion, simply because you want to make your parents or other authority figures angry. True intimacy is not about everyone else. The pursuit of the one you love to be with the one you love is simply about you and them, because you desire to be with them – where they are – in their presence – sharing each moment as it comes.

In complete opposition to the powers that be, the woman clarifies something important for herself in chapter 8. Even though her male relatives feel they need to make decisions for her and locked her away from the world to protect their own reputation through her virtue, she stands up and speaks for herself. Her vineyard – whether a literal vineyard or a figurative one, speaking of her body – is hers to defend and hers to give, not theirs. She is responsible; she speaks for herself; she decides for herself; she does not need someone else to defend her, nor do it for her. She is strong and capable, and able to stand on her own. Right here, we see one of the ultimate signs of preparedness for an intimate relationship. She was ready because she knew herself, honored herself, and stood up for herself enough to know what she wants. That makes her a wall and a fortress of her own making, her own tower. A true woman does not need to be locked up in one, no!! She is one herself, a pillar of strength and fortitude in the world.

Entering intimacy is a choice we make for ourselves.

No one can force us to be intimate with someone else, because intimacy is something that finds us. People can be married, they can be together, they can be arranged, but if intimacy finds them not, they will not experience true intimacy. This woman's decision to stand up and decide for herself what she will or will not do shows that this relationship was her own choice. What an amazing stand for her – and for all women!

When we desire to enter an intimate relationship with someone, we must be responsible for ourselves. We must be able to speak for ourselves and know what we ourselves want. Nobody is in this relationship but the couple and nobody can communicate the essentials of self but those two people to one another. Every one of us needs to have the assurance of character and the being that God has created us to be to know just how to interact in intimacy.

Intimacy is something to be experienced, felt, touched, and known. This means it doesn't come with a handbook, nor a series and set guidelines of rules. Intimacy is a different dynamic from anything else we've experienced prior. It doesn't play games, and it doesn't rely on everyone else to define it for us. Intimacy is a step into maturity, and it changes us. Intimate relationships are truly a sign of knowing oneself and coming to a greater knowledge of one's purpose in life. As the Song of Solomon makes the relationship sound extremely desirable, it is something we should desire. It shows we are past the childish games of our youth and experimentation with boundaries and limits, and are ready to have something real and true, with the potential to last.

The same is true when we begin to pursue God genuinely – for ourselves. The patriarchal presence in our own personal lives often sounds a lot like our parents and church leaders, who told us we had to go to church for no other reason than it was an obligation. So many in this world have run from the things of God because someone made them pursue a concept of God and a concept of religion when they were children. Whatever this concept might have been, the messages many received were contradictory or confusing. In a natural state, many rebel against the concepts they were raised with. Just as with an intimate relationship, when we seek God, God finds us as much as we find Him. We fall into a place where we seek God and love Him for who we know Him to be, not for who someone else told us He was. Intimacy with God shows a maturity within us – a readiness to know and love Him beyond ritual, religion, and external actions – but just know Him, as He is.

It's obvious the systems that exist have hurt us in more ways than one. The controlling rules and regulations that often define and shape our entire ways of viewing ourselves and relationships keep us from the intimacy we, as human beings, both desire and need for survival and success in this world. As we continue to look at various dynamics and dimensions of intimacy found in the Song of Solomon, take some steps back and do some examination of your own life and your own issues. Where is intimacy desired? What issues exist? What rules and regulations are keeping you from intimacy's potential? What rules are keeping you from a greater sense of knowing yourself, and your ability to make your own decisions? How can you challenge the system by changing yourself? Making changes starts from within. If we will only see our own call to experience what the lovers had in the Song of Solomon, our own abilities for intimacy will change, grow, and mature, as well.

CHAPTER 3

Desire and Sex

Key verses

- **Verses 2:3-5:** *Like an apple tree among the trees of the forest is my lover among the young men. I delight to sit in his shade, and his fruit is sweet to my taste. He has taken me to the banquet hall, and his banner over me is love. Strengthen me with raisins, refresh me with apples, for I am faint with love.*

- **Verse 2:13:** *The fig tree forms its early fruit; the blossoming vines spread their fragrance. Arise, come, my darling; my beautiful one, come with me.*

- **Verse 2:16:** *My lover is mine and I am his; he browses among the lilies.*

- **Verse 4:7:** *All beautiful you are, my darling; there is no flaw in you.*

- **Verse 5:10:** *My lover is radiant and ruddy, outstanding among ten thousand.*

- **Verse 5:9:** *How is your beloved better than others, most beautiful of women? How is your beloved better than others, that you charge us so?*

- **Verse 5:16:** *"His mouth is sweetness itself; he is altogether lovely. This is my lover, this my friend, O daughters of Jerusalem.*

- **Verse 6:3:** *I am my lover's and my lover is mine; he browses among the lilies.*

- **Verse 7:10:** *I belong to my lover, and his desire is for me.*

Words and phrases to know

- **Apple tree:** From the Hebrew word *tappuwach* which means "apple, apple tree."[1]

- **Sit in his shade:** From two Hebrew words: *yashab* which means "to dwell, remain, sit, abide;"[2] and *tsel* which means "shadow, shade."[3]

- **Fruit:** From the Hebrew word *peiry* which means "fruit."[4]

- **Sweet:** From the Hebrew word *mathuwq* which means "sweet; sweetness; pleasant thing."[5]

- **Banquet hall:** From two Hebrew words: *yayin* which means "wine"[6] and *bayith* which means "house; place; receptacle; home, house as in containing a family; household, family; household affairs; inward (metaphorical); temple (adverb); on the inside (preposition); within."[7]

- **Banner:** From the Hebrew word *degel* which means "banner, standard."[8]

- **Love:** From the Hebrew word *'ahabah* which means "love; God's love to His people."[9]

- **Embraces:** From the Hebrew word *chabaq* which means "to embrace, clasp."[10]

- **Winter:** From the Hebrew word *cethav* which means "winter, rainy season."[11]

- **Rain:** From the Hebrew word *geshem* which means "rain, shower."[12]

- **Flowers:** From the Hebrew word *nitstsan* which means "blossom."[13]

- **Season of singing:** From two Hebrew words: *'eth* which means "time"[14] and *zamiyr* or *zamir* or "zamirah" which means "song, psalm."[15]

- **Cooing of doves:** From two Hebrew words: *qowl* or *qol* which means "voice, sound, noise; lightness, frivolity"[16] and *towr* or *tor* which means "dove, turtledove."[17]

- **Blossoming vines:** From two Hebrew words: *gephen* which means "vine, vine tree"[18] and *cemadar* which means "grape blossom, grape bud."[19]

- **Gilead:** From the Hebrew word *Gil'ad* which means "rocky region; a mountainous region bound on the west by the Jordan, on the north by Bashan, on the east by the Arabian Plateau, and on the south by Moab and Ammon; sometimes called Mount Gilead or the Land of Gilead or just Gilead. Divided into north and south Gilead; a city (with the prefix Jabesh); the people of the region; a son of Machir and grandson of Manasseh; father of Jephthah; a Gadite."[20]

- **Tower of David:** From two Hebrew words: *migdalah* which means "tower (feminine)"[21] and *David* which means "David (beloved); youngest son of Jesse and second king of Israel."[22]

- **Mountain of myrrh:** From two Hebrew words: *har* which means "hill, mountain, hill country, mount;"[23] and *more*, which means "myrrh."[24]

- **Hill of incense:** From two Hebrew words: *gib'ah* which means "hill"[25] and *lebownah* which means "frankincense."[26]

- **Flaw:** From the Hebrew word *m'uwm* which means "blemish, spot, defect."[27]

- **Outstanding:** From the Hebrew word *dagal* which means "to look, behold; to carry a banner or standard, to set a standard."[28]

- **Lebanon:** From the Hebrew word *Lebanown* which means "whiteness; a wooded mountain range on the northern border of Israel."[29]

- **Friend:** From the Hebrew word *'reh* or *reya'* which means "friend, companion, fellow, another person."[30]

- **Desire:** From the Hebrew word *teshuwqah* which means "desire, longing, craving."[31]

- **Mandrakes:** From the Hebrew word *duwday* which means "mandrake, love apple; as exciting sexual desire, and favoring procreation."[32]

- **Roused:** From the Hebrew word *'uwr* which means "to rouse oneself, awake, awaken, excite."[33]

Lust. Desire. Sex. Attraction. What's acceptable in intimacy? What's not? The modern church takes the issues of sex, lust, desire, and attraction to extremes unheard in times prior. Some groups pretend people do not experience desire and sex, while others go to the extreme of sex seminars and other often quipped advice, given to their congregations in the name of helping marriages and relationships.

As with all things, there must be a balance in here between every presented extreme. Unfortunately, I don't see a lot of balance on these matters. Today's ministers attempt to provide guidance on these subjects to their followers. The problem is that most ministers offer advice and information based on their own personal perspectives on these issues, instead of seeing what the Scriptures have to offer as pertains therein to them. Due to societal discomforts, talk of these issues has ministers in a spin as to what should or should not be said, with the result often coming out all wrong.

Sex, desire, attraction, and physical drives are an uncomfortable topic for many. The reality is, however, that if we encourage people to develop intimate relationships, these things are often a part of such a relationship. If we ourselves cannot talk about them in an objective manner, we can't encourage couples to discuss these matters in a personal way together. Because sex, desire, and attraction are all forms of communication, they are things we need to be able to communicate about through objective relationship advice and encouragement.

Intimacy is represented sexually because it is both an

entering and a receiving; it is where we go into the recesses of purpose and depth – to the deepest part – to receive the most powerful revelation of pleasure and life-purpose. If we cannot discuss things which pertain to sex, we cannot discuss and understand intimacy in a way that will be relatable to those who seek our advice and perspective on these topics. It will also hurt our own ability to be intimate, and to relate in an intimate way in our own lives.

The major thing modern relationships and modern relationship advice pertaining to intimacy lacks is a sense of respectful privacy. This is because we are not approaching the advice we give from the perspective of intimacy. If a couple dwells together in intimacy, there needs to be a communication about desire and sex rather than a list of dos and don'ts purported by the church. A respect for intimacy must be maintained when it comes to advice about desire and sex. If we approach these matters in this way, people who seek will come to a place where they have answers instead of questions.

Desire

Lover

How beautiful you are, my darling!
Oh, how beautiful!
Your eyes behind your veil are doves.
Your hair is like a flock of goats
descending from Mount Gilead.
Your teeth are like a flock of sheep just shorn,
coming up from the washing.
Each has its twin;
not one of them is alone.
Your lips are like a scarlet ribbon;
your mouth is lovely.

Your temples behind your veil
are like the halves of a pomegranate.
Your neck is like the tower of David,
built with elegance;
on it hang a thousand shields,
all of them shields of warriors.
Your two breasts are like two fawns,
like twin fawns of a gazelle
that browse among the lilies.
Until the day breaks
and the shadows flee,
I will go to the mountain of myrrh
and to the hill of incense.
All beautiful you are, my darling;
there is no flaw in you.
(4:1-7)

Beloved

My lover is radiant and ruddy,
outstanding among ten thousand.
His head is purest gold;
his hair is wavy
and black as a raven.
His eyes are like doves
by the water streams,
washed in milk,
mounted like jewels.
His cheeks are like beds of spice
yielding perfume.
His lips are like lilies
dripping with myrrh.
His arms are rods of gold
set with chrysolite.
His body is like polished ivory
decorated with sapphires.

His legs are pillars of marble
set on bases of pure gold.
His appearance is like Lebanon,
choice as its cedars.
His mouth is sweetness itself;
he is altogether lovely.
This is my lover, this my friend,
O daughters of Jerusalem.
(5:10-16)

The word "desire" connotes something in most people's minds. To some, "desire" is all about physical sex, void of connection. Some people reduce the word "desire" to being all about someone's wish and seeking to fulfill a personal wish. Still, some people think desires are something secretive, something that people should never discuss, as if they are long and forgotten dreams of a distant past.

"Desire" can be said to be a little bit of everything mentioned above, but it is, in its essence, far more than just what is mentioned here. It is more intense than wishing, far more serious than a distant dream, and definitely something to be discussed. It is not all about sex, although one can desire to be with someone else in a physical sense. Those who fall on the asexual perspective prove that desire – as they may desire several things in their lives – is about far more than just physical sex. Desire is, above all things, a pursuit of one's life. Desire can apply to any and every area of one's existence: we can desire to do things spiritually, emotionally, physically, mentally, or emotionally.

Desire is different from lust, which is simply an intense, motivating drive to acquire something. Behind lust, we find the motivator to be power, rather than love or something substantial. Lust is fleeting, while desire doesn't pass quite so easily. Desire does not seek to possess or conquer, but rather, to be with. It can be overwhelming, but at the same time, desire within us knows something we may not cognitively know: it knows where the answer to our satisfaction ultimately lies.

Desire is also different from attraction, although it is related to it. Any one of us can walk down a street and pass someone and find them attractive. Noticing and appreciating the beauty God has created in the form of another person is just that: a notice and an appreciation. It is not lustful, nor is it desire. Attraction is a key facet to continuation of the species (we won't want to procreate if we can't stand to look at anyone); therefore, God created us to notice one another. Attraction is not sinful...however, it is also not desire. While people who desire one another do find one another attractive, there is more to desire than physical attraction. Desire goes beyond attraction (which in the New Testament era was identified as *eros* in the Greek) into love (defined as *agape*), as each partner seeks the highest possible good and connection for the other.

Desire is about our intentions, wants, needs, and interactions as people. Desire reveals the innermost nature of our being: who we are, what is important to us, who we want to be, and where we want to go. It pertains to where we seek our greatest satisfaction and purpose in life. In essence, our desires are an extension of us.

In the context we are discussing here, desire relates to a desire for intimacy and to pursue an intimate relationship. The couple in the Song of Solomon wrote extensively about their desires. If one doesn't read the Scriptures properly, they can sound shallow and superficial, like all they seek to discuss is about things on the surface - for example, how the other person looks to them. It also seems like this is all they keep talking about. If we look closer, however, the couple is trying to explain something that is eternal in experience, but personal to them, because they are the ones who are experiencing it. The couple is expressing desire through the things they can identify and see in the natural realm. Even though they are talking about the physical, they are expressing the eternal in their words. This couple truly desired each other beyond what they could describe, so they tried to describe everything. Have you ever had someone in your life that you just love "everything" about? All right, maybe you don't love everything about them, but there are so many things about them, you simply can't list them all? That's what is going on here in the Song of Solomon. The couple sees so many things in each other that are desirable, they want to tell of them.

The reality of desire, however, is that it is more than just simple attributes. Even though there may be many things that we love about someone, that doesn't mean we desire them. Desire is something that in many ways manifests in the natural realm, but it begins in the spiritual realm. Desire is something spiritual; it echoes our longing for the divine. It is our essential cry out of the isolation and bondage of sin to become one with someone or something else. We seek to find something so desirable, yet only satisfied in a complete oneness with what we seek – ultimately, God. This means that the pursuit of desire-based intimacy also leads us to a place of holiness. Each partner makes the other better, brings out the best, challenges inconsistencies, encourages, corrects, and polishes out the rough edges and spots within the other's personality. True intimacy is about oneself, and also about the other, as well. It is in this balance that we find the desire to become better – to become better as individuals and also more complete as one – in the striving for unity and purpose. In this instance, intimacy builds up the ultimate in possible holiness as each partner dies to themselves for the good of the other…rising once again to new life in the love they share together.

Where our desires lie tell a lot about the whole of who we are as people. There are just some people in this life that we love forever, no matter what happens, who comes and goes, or how things change. These are the people we need to pay attention to because God is telling us something about them, and about our connection to them, in that simple desire to love and be with them. We can't explain it, it doesn't make sense to anyone (maybe even to us ourselves) – but somehow, that love, that desire, finds its rest in the bond of intimacy.

The lovers in the Song of Solomon have found this rest for their desires in one another. As is expected, the lovers desire one another's attention, time, and companionship. With all things closely intimate, the couple's desire turns to their physical expression, through sex.

Setting ourselves aright

Beloved

Like an apple tree among the trees of the forest
is my lover among the young men.
I delight to sit in his shade,
and his fruit is sweet to my taste.
He has taken me to the banquet hall,
and his banner over me is love.
Strengthen me with raisins,
refresh me with apples,
for I am faint with love.
His left arm is under my head,
and his right arm embraces me.
Daughters of Jerusalem, I charge you
by the gazelles and by the does of the field:
Do not arouse or awaken love
until it so desires.
Listen! My lover!
Look! Here he comes,
leaping across the mountains,
bounding over the hills.
My lover is like a gazelle or a young stag.
Look! There he stands behind our wall,
gazing through the windows,
peering through the lattice.
My lover spoke and said to me,
"Arise, my darling,

my beautiful one, and come with me.
See! The winter is past;
the rains are over and gone.
Flowers appear on the earth;
the season of singing has come,
the cooing of doves
is heard in our land.
The fig tree forms its early fruit;
the blossoming vines spread their fragrance.
Arise, come, my darling;
my beautiful one, come with me."
(2:3-13)

Beloved

Awake, north wind,
and come, south wind!
Blow on my garden,
that its fragrance may spread abroad.
Let my lover come into his garden

and taste its choice fruits.
(4:16)

(Related Bible references: Hebrews 13:4, 1 Corinthians 7:1-5, Psalm 23:5, 1 John 4:8, 1 John 4:18, 1 Corinthians 13:11, Revelation 2:4-5)

The Song of Solomon defies conventional relationship stereotypes. I believe this is one of the reasons it is so ignored and downplayed by patriarchal systems. Patriarchy is not absent from the book, as we have already discussed; but it is also hard-fought by the woman in its pages. The woman, the beloved, is often the pursuer, as we can see here. She is not merely the recipient of affections. She doesn't play "hard to get." She is interested in the lover, wants to be with him, and is unashamed of her desire toward him. She is not just an object of desire, but one who desires. Her desires are given as much credibility and reality as the man's are. The book never presents her behavior as shameful or regrettable. The drive for sex is not exclusive to men and the drive for love and intimacy, not exclusive to women. The most universal ideal for both men and women is to find all three in one.

Achieving this seems more difficult than ever. A persistent loneliness haunts many people in our modern day and age. With more technology to reach out and contact others, we seem lost and abandoned in our technology. One of the greatest disservices society has done to relationships is turning marriage into a status symbol. We can see this present throughout the Bible, where women are seen more as status symbols and achievements as progenitors than individuals with a God-given purpose. As a result of the politics between men and women, most people approach relationships with an attitude of dissatisfaction and caution. We settle, allowing society to dictate the terms of our relationships. We lose our individuality in the hopes of conformity. Most of us within the human condition spend time pursuing people who are not interested in us. We try to attract attention (the wrong attention) from the opposite sex, hoping someone will come along and desire us as a result of the attention we attempt to generate. We forget that God's anointing upon us makes us attractive. There is no reason for a man or a woman to run around without self-respect and dignity. The Word clearly voices that desire and self-respect are not opposites.

Society and religion alike have a way of shaming women, disguising that shame as self-respect. It is not self-respecting to go through life with unmet and unsatisfied desire. It is also not dignified to go through life with an unhealthy attitude toward sexuality. Never exploring physical desire leaves an essential component of intimacy out of the experiential equation. The Song of Solomon proves the ideal woman is all of the above: she knows who she is, what she's got, how to present it, how it can benefit her and those in her life, how valuable she is, and both how desirable she is and the depths of her own desire. There is nothing wrong or ungodly about any of this. On the contrary, a godly woman carries with her both desire and passion: spiritually, physically, emotionally, and sensually.

Even within her desire, the woman present in the Song of Solomon maintains a pursuant level of class. She doesn't just stand on the street corner in sexually suggestive clothing and offer herself to every man that comes along. She's not looking for someone who is shallow and insincere. Her interest was toward a man who was equally interested in her. What we find in her is a balance of sexuality, sensuality, respectability, and common sense. No, she doesn't have to pretend she is not interested, but she also doesn't have to put herself so far out there that she becomes obnoxious about it. We find the answer that pretending not to be interested in sex or pretending not to experience desire is not what builds a good relationship.

The concept of "hard to get" is destructive to relationships. Even though society has told women to refrain from displaying interest in men as a pursuit to manipulate them into marriage, playing this game introduces just that – manipulation – into a relationship. It conveys the message that a woman is willing to use emotional distance to get what she wants, at all costs. This is dishonest. If two people are interested in one another, that should be acknowledged, not foregone in the hopes a man will pursue a woman into a misguided concept of submission. Relationships should not be pursued against another's will, and "hard to get" gives the impression that force is, in actuality, a proper dynamic for intimacy. It also causes men to misread signals. If someone's advances are unwarranted, that should not be confused with a dishonest mixed signal. No needs to mean no, and yes needs to mean yes. This is the only way clear communication can be established in a relationship.

The metaphorical language of the Song of Solomon codes the forward nature of her desires. While she put it tastefully, her desire was to indulge herself orally with her lover. She wanted to sit in the shade of his body, using her mouth to pleasure him sexually. In chapter 4 verse 16, she talks of him doing the same to her. This nullifies and answers several questions many church members have about oral sex and sexual gratification using the sense of taste. Throughout history, such a practice has been regarded as filthy, uncouth, and even sinful for one reason or another. The Word states different. If it is a desired action (and the Word does depict it here as a desire), there is nothing wrong with doing it, performing it, or giving or receiving it – neither for a man, nor for a woman, nor for anyone else. Scripture reminds us that the marriage bed is undefiled (Hebrews 13:4). This means the activity that takes place there, given the relationship is both mutual and consensual, is a private matter between those in it. This also raises the differences in interest and preference as pertains to sexual relationships. More than anything, I get many questions as pertains to what is or is not "acceptable" during sex. The only prohibition that exists in a couple's relationship is sexual violence. Not everybody likes or enjoys the same things in a relationship. No matter what someone's preferences may be, there should be a haste, an interest, and a longing for sexual pleasure and gratification, however it is sought, in a relationship (1 Corinthians 7:1-5). I believe this passage reminds us of the essence in remaining non-judgmental when it comes to private expressions of intimacy – as well as remaining open to variety, as long as we are comfortable with what we seek to do.

The honest way in which the woman expresses herself reminds us of the importance of sexual discussion in relationships. Too often, sex is treated as a reward or a weapon among popular culture. We give the message that if someone is "very good" at giving us what we want – whether it's a relationship, money, security, power, or status – we will allow them to have sex with us. This has created a dishonesty surrounding sex and sexual relationships. It has especially made it a taboo topic, even when a couple is in a sexual relationship. Sexual discussion needs to remain an open option between couples. When intimate partners shut down discussion on this matter, they shut down discussion in other areas of the relationship, as well. It is not particularly appropriate to discuss preferences, likes, and dislikes with everyone you know – but it is important to be able to discuss these things with the one you are most intimate with.

The chapter progresses from very intimate aspects of the couple's relationship to more public ones. The desire of another creates the desire to spend time together in varied activities. Couples who are truly intimate know they do not need to spend every moment together but do desire to spend that quality time with one another. The terminology, "going to the banquet hall," has a dual representation. Christian circles today debate the issue of dating. There are so-called leaders who tell women to stay home and wait for the one whom God chooses for them to appear. Unless God drops someone out of the sky onto their cars, there is no conceivable way these women will find someone. Christian women and men alike who are single should not feel unduly pressured to go to places that may create discomfort or inappropriate circumstances, such as bars or clubs that may pose a danger. Christian men and women, however, should never shy away from being social or from dating. There are many purposes dating serves that do not pertain to sex with multiple partners. Dating gives us the opportunity to get to know a potential mate, discover likes and dislikes, as well as suitability to another. Dating also serves the intensive purpose of learning how to interact with the opposite sex and in a relationship context with others, how to handle situations that arise between the sexes, and to discover what a person seeks in a mate. Dating also provides fun in a social environment, and an opportunity to try new things. All these experiences are of benefit to the Christian believer, no matter what stage of life one may be at.

Dating is also just as important for the couple that has found each other as the couple who is just getting to know one another. Since dating is a social experience, coupled with getting to know one another, dating provides even the most experienced couple an opportunity to know their mate in a different way or learn something new about them. Dating and social outing as a couple proves there is no shame in a relationship. Intimacy reveals the deepest part of another person, and social outing brings forth the balance to intimacy. Relationships based on secrets don't lead to intimacy, they lead to secrecy. Solid relationships should never be based in shame or forced to remain hidden. A good man of God and a good woman of God will be proud to be seen with their significant other, anywhere it demands.

How are we about our relationship with God and public relevance? Do we make our faith known, or are we ashamed of God? The difference between secrecy and intimacy can be seen no clearer than it can as one's relationship with God. If you are afraid to make your faith known, to stand up for your faith, to spend time with Him, even in the public place of His temple, your relationship with God is not intimate, it's a secret. It is not God's will that our relationship with Him be kept silent. We should never, ever be ashamed of God. If people in our lives don't understand that relationship, that is their problem, not ours. God brings us forth to His incredible banquet, where His banner over us is love. A banner is a public event, not a private one – set in the midst of our enemies (Psalm 23:5). God is never ashamed of us, and we should never, ever be ashamed of Him.

Being faint with love literally means being "lovesick." All of us remember our first and early relationships, where all we could think about was the person we were involved with. They were our every thought, feeling, and pursuit. We found it hard to focus on other things, such as work, school, or family life. The daydreams and thoughts at night always travelled to that beloved, special person. There was a constant curiosity about what was going on and what was to come.

We use the term "first love" today to indicate someone who was the first person in our lives to be the first male or female we interacted with on a romantic level. Some might define a "first love" as a first serious relationship. The understanding of having a first love goes beyond just the romantic dynamics, however. There was an excitement and expectation with the relationship that we never experience again, especially the longer we are involved with others in a romantic context. We give of ourselves in a way with firsts that is innocent: we do not fear being hurt, we do not fear lack of trust – all we know is that moment, that first, that experience. As we go along and learn more about our likes, dislikes, and interests, the raw experimentation of first love fades away, into a more precise purpose in relationship. We also deal with hurts, pains, and violations that cause us to close off, distrust, developing barriers to intimacy. What our later relationships carry from our first within us is the promise of firsts with that person – a first date, first kiss, first dance, and first promise of intimacy – that spans through each situation. The initial excitement we feel, the "faintness of love," is always the same in that it always comes.

When we love someone, they should easily come to memory. The thoughts of them should never be so far and so distant, we forget their place, inspiration, and love in our lives. If someone is not so easily accessible by memory – or we simply do not miss or desire to bring them to memory – they are not serving a purpose of love in our lives. Relationships do go through stages, but love should always be a focal point of it all, in both recollection and response.

First love also can pertain to this initial stage of a relationship – literally every relationship goes through its period of "first love," when the relationship is new. Every relationship carries that stamp of "first love," whereby we may come in with caution, but we are still experiencing the newness of the experience. That newness makes everything alive and different: our senses are heightened because we are experiencing love all over again, yet for the very first time. This is why the Bible talks of "first love" in the context of the Lord – the church in Ephesus, mentioned in Revelation (Revelation 2:4-5) was spoken of as leaving its "first love," the Lord. If we are believers, our first love should always be the Lord, because it is by the Lord that our lives began again. Thanks to God, we have a repeated opportunity to get things right. As He is love (1 John 4:8, 1 John 4:18), His love is that from which all our love radiates. We learn how to love from God, and we learn intimacy as we walk with Him in a powerful way. The relationships we have may come and go, they often change, and they will even hurt at times – some more than others. Still, when we are in the Lord, and He is our first love, we are always able to bring Him to remembrance...His Word to our focus...and His love to our lives. When we are in Christ, we can always love again, because His love moves in us, and His life causes our being to stir. Despite our hurts or wounds, we can always experience the newness of love.

In love, in its newness and experience, we should experience the embrace of love. Our lover or beloved should be one trustworthy enough to catch us when we fall. In life, people falter. We go through highs and lows, pains and joys. Intimate relationships represent a place of comfort and security. It is an intimate partner's role to stand strong when all the other desires to do is fall apart. Intimacy brings with it a powerful sense of hope, possibility, and restoration, even in the midst of difficulty or despair. This reminds us of God's true embrace to us: His ability to pull us out of any pit or difficult situation, inspire hope and faith within us, and bring us to a different place.

The Song of Solomon brings us much practical wisdom about relationships and intimacy, and how the two interconnect. One of the most basic pieces of advice it gives to us is the practical advice: Don't arouse or awaken love until it desires. We've all heard the slogans that nauseate us: "Wait for your Boaz/Ruth!" "Don't just settle for Mr./Ms. Right Now, wait for Mr./Ms. Right!" It is much simpler to follow the advice of the Scriptures, and not attempt to arouse or awaken love until it desires. What is the difference? In the realm of advice, the words given indicate that the individual trying to find a right relationship is doing something wrong. As we discussed earlier, there is nothing wrong with dating or socializing in pursuit of a relationship. What is wrong is when one tries to force themselves into feeling a certain way about someone as they try to pursue a relationship. It is a mistake to enter a long-term or marital arrangement when the desire of love just is not there. We cannot force love, nor desire – not by arrangement, social custom, hopes, prayers, or wishes – it is something that just comes, as it will.

This means we must be sensitive to the states of life people choose to live in for themselves. Marriage is not for everybody. Just because someone is single, that does not mean there is something wrong with them. Not wanting to marry – whether due to the current phase of one's life or never wanting to marry – is valid. Having standards is not a bad thing. Waiting until love finds someone is the right thing to do – not the wrong thing. We should honor those who make the commitment to wait on long-term relationships rather than pressuring them into making relationship mistakes. As people, we need to step back and let love happen. This gives us three main points for relationship viewpoints, which cover all the major relationships one may have to someone in a relationship:

- Unless someone is in a situation that is somehow threatening to their well-being, we need to refrain from being overly involved or opinionated about their relationship. People need room to figure out love for themselves within their own relationship dynamics. Unsolicited advice creates a situation where people go the opposite way they should – and can in many instances, detour far from where they start.

- When it comes to relationships, people around us can give useful advice. I don't mean to suggest that we should never get advice, nor that we should never talk about problems with others. However, in the end, we must make the decision ourselves. If something is right, we can tell that by the situations and circumstances as well as the Holy Spirit speaking something to us.

- Pressuring people into relationships for the wrong reasons – their age, their situation in life, etc. – is contrary to the principle of letting relationships develop on their own. When a relationship is ready to move forward, the people in that relationship know and recognize that.

There is so much to be said for the simple things in a relationship. With so many obstacles, opinions, and people who try to interfere in the natural and spiritual process, the simple, little, and even innocent aspects of a relationship can bring great blessings. The woman in this passage rejoices at the sight and idea of her lover coming to her, even though all they could have was a simple peek over the fence or a dialogue at the window. The simplicity in this is rooted in the beauty of a new start. Singing of the promise that winter is past and the earth would now bloom and blossom in springtime represents the power of newness. Many people go through so many emotional and spiritual winters throughout their lives. The end of relationships, periods of loneliness, emotional distance, turmoil and stress all create "winter" periods. Things seem bleak, life seems dead, and the cold and distance around us seems larger than life. When we come to a place of simplicity with both ourselves and others – and are starting something new – we can feel God's presence and promise with us. In the simplicity of relationship dynamics, we are excited, purposed, ready, and full of promise. We know more is to come, and we anticipate that newness of things never done before and things soon to come. Even if we have done those things many times with another or others, we still walk that fine line of uncertainty and eagerness. It is new, to be experienced again for the very first time.

The same newness should apply in our relationship with God – but seldom does. When we are first believers, we are eager and excited to learn about the things of God. Being with God is an exciting experience. As we grow in our walk with Him, we don't approach God in the same way that we used to. In some ways, this is a sign of maturity. The Bible teaches us that when we are children, we approach things as children; but when we become adults, we put aside childish ways (1 Corinthians 13:11). We should gain a deeper knowledge and understanding of God, gained through years of relationship and intimacy with Him. This is not always the result, however. Many people start to see God as nothing more than an obligation – something to move through our days and out of the way – as they move on to things deemed more important or relevant. Seeing God in this way means one does not have a good, impacting, and life-changing relationship with Him.

Being with God should always be approached as a new experience. Whether we are praying, studying, praising, worshipping, or simply sitting with Him in His presence, we should always see it as a springtime experience. If approached right, it will pull us out of any winter we may experience and launch us right into spring. In that place, God can renew something already placed within us, or bring us into a new season. When He calls us unto Him, we should move with Him, excited about where God seeks to take us.

I am my beloved's...

Beloved

My lover is mine and I am his;
he browses among the lilies.
Until the day breaks
and the shadows flee,
turn, my lover,
and be like a gazelle
or like a young stag
on the rugged hills.
(2:16-17)

Friends

How is your beloved better than others,
most beautiful of women?
How is your beloved better than others,
that you charge us so?
(5:9)

Lover

My lover has gone down to his garden,
to the beds of spices,
to browse in the gardens
and to gather lilies.
I am my lover's and my lover is mine;
he browses among the lilies.
(6:2-3)

Lover

I belong to my lover,
and his desire is for me.
Come, my lover, let us go to the countryside,

let us spend the night in the villages.
Let us go early to the vineyards
to see if the vines have budded,
if their blossoms have opened,
and if the pomegranates are in bloom—
there I will give you my love.
The mandrakes send out their fragrance,
and at our door is every delicacy,
both new and old,
that I have stored up for you, my lover.
(7:10-13)

Friends

Who is this coming up from the desert
leaning on her lover?

Beloved

Under the apple tree I roused you;
there your mother conceived you,
there she who was in labor gave you birth.
(8:5)

It is not uncommon to meet people who consider themselves as 'belonging' to one another when they are in a relationship. This is a fine precept, as long as it is a mutual understanding. When intimacy is present in a relationship, it draws exclusivity between the two. There is oneness present, where the two understand each other and the meaning they both have to one another. This is indicative of a possessiveness, realizing the relationship is special and unique. What intimate partners have with one another, they do not have with everyone else in their lives.

It is a true shame that the language of intimacy has

been perverted by many into a language of abuse. This is Satan's deception, trying to draw people into a fear of intimacy because they associate it with mistreatment. Let us never confuse exclusivity with isolation or degradation. People in relationships should not ever be considered the property of the other, as something to use or abuse. Intimacy does not create abuse, it creates purpose and closeness. The closeness of intimacy draws one to spend extended time, hours, days, and enjoyment on end, as the two grow and learn from one another.

To whom do you belong? Everyone in the world belongs to someone. We either belong to the Lord, or we belong to the enemy. There isn't a middle ground. Can you truly say that you belong to the Lord, the One Who loves you beyond measure? Have you attended to the little foxes that challenge, change, or damage that relationship? Are you spending time with Him, working to make that relationship deeper and closer? Are you pursuing other things (other gods) that compromise your relationship with God? Wherever you are, God is calling out to you, seeking to be your first love, one that you spend your time with and develop a unique bond with. He seeks Your time and Your hope. Have you answered Him?

CHAPTER 4

Sensuality and Experience

Key verses

- **Verses 1:2:-3**: *Let him kiss me with the kisses of his mouth-- for your love is more delightful than wine. Pleasing is the fragrance of your perfumes; your name is like perfume poured out. No wonder the maidens love you!*

- **Verses 1:12-14**: *While the king was at his table, my perfume spread its fragrance. My lover is to me a sachet of myrrh resting between my breasts. My lover is to me a cluster of henna blossoms from the vineyards of En Gedi.*

- **Verses 4:11-12**: *Your lips drop sweetness as the honeycomb, my bride; milk and honey are under your tongue. The fragrance of your garments is like that of Lebanon. You are a garden locked up, my sister, my bride; you are a spring enclosed, a sealed fountain.*

- **Verse 4:16**: *Awake, north wind, and come, south wind! Blow on my garden, that its fragrance may* *spread abroad. Let my lover come into his garden and taste its choice fruits.*

- **Verse 5:1:** *I am come into my garden, my sister, my spouse: I have gathered my myrrh with my spice; I have eaten my honeycomb with my honey; I have drunk my wine with my milk: eat, O friends; drink, yea, drink abundantly, O beloved.*

- **Verse 6:10:** *Who is this that appears like the dawn, fair as the moon, bright as the sun, majestic as the stars in procession?*

- **Verse 6:13:** *Come back, come back, O Shulammite; come back, come back, that we may gaze on you! Why would you gaze on the Shulammite as on the dance of Mahanaim?*

Words and phrases to know

- **Kiss:** From the Hebrew word *nashaq* which means "to put together, kiss; to handle, be equipped with"[1]

- **Fragrance:** From the Hebrew word *'reyach* which means "scent, fragrance, aroma, odor."[2]

- **Perfume:** From the Hebrew word *shemen* which means "fat, oil."[3]

- **Young Women:** From the Hebrew word *'almah* which means "virgin, young woman."[4]

- **Chambers:** From the Hebrew word *'cheder* which means "chamber, room, parlor, innermost or inward part, within."[5]

- **Darling:** From the Hebrew word *rayah* which means "attendant maidens, companion"[6]

- **Sweetness:** From the Hebrew word *nopheth* which means "flowing honey, honey from the comb, a dropping down, honey, honeycomb."[7]

- **Garments:** From the Hebrew word *salmah* which means "garment, outer garment, wrapper, mantle."[8]

- **Sister:** From the Hebrew word *'achowth* which means "sister."[9]

- **Bride:** From the Hebrew word *kallah* which means "bride, daughter-in-law."[10]

- **Garden:** From the Hebrew word *gan* which means "garden, enclosure."[11]

- **Shulammite:** From the Hebrew word *Shuwlammiyth* which means "the perfect or the peaceful; the heroine lover of the Song of Solomon (Songs)."[12]

- **Gaze:** From the Hebrew word *chazah* which means "to see, perceive, look, behold, prophecy, provide."[13]

- **Dance of Mahanaim:** From two Hebrew words: *mechowlah* which means "dancing, dance"[14] and *machaneh* which means "encampment, camp."[15]

In Christianity, we hear a lot about the flesh and the Spirit, and the war between the two. People who do not live as they should are considered "carnal" or "fleshly." It is often said they live exclusively according to their senses – what they can perceive in a natural way. The contrast we give for those who live by the Spirit is the opposite – they are said to live by that which they cannot see, and divine principles govern their actions. Those who are spiritual are said to have no connection to their senses, but somehow operate by a distant perception. Those who are carnal are said to be all about what they physically sense, and not at all about what they perceive.

At the same time, Christians today also receive the message that their faith life is a system of belief and material reward. Believers are taught to use the life of the Spirit to get what they want in the material. Many prominent teachers encourage their followers to use their faith to generate material things for themselves. We are told that if we just use our faith, we can have all the things we desire, including those things which we can perceive by the senses.

It's obvious we are given a double message here: In one breath, we are told sensuality is bad, but in the next, we are told to use our faith to obtain it. What I believe is more prevalent than anything is a sort of selective sensuality: we make physical sensuality, specifically that which relates to sex, or tangible contact with other human beings, inherently wrong. Then we make other material things perceived by the senses acceptable, such as getting a car, a house, or money. This dividing line way of thinking divides the individual Christian. On one hand, they believe they receive tangibly by faith, but on the other hand, they believe everything they perceive sensually to be evil. What does this mean for the believer? If this is the case, how do we experience life? How do we experience God? Is everything perceived by the senses bad, or is there a context to it? If sensory experience is inherently evil, then why do we have senses in the first place?

The Song of Solomon makes it clear that the battle between flesh and the Spirit is not as clean-cut as some make it today. It is also not quite as complicated as we make it. In fact, the book downright challenges the notion that what we perceive via the senses is all inherently evil.

What this important book does is provide a grounding point for us in explaining the spiritual through the sensual. Sensuality is not inherently evil; it is how sensuality is used, perceived, and controlled that makes a difference. It is important we understand sensuality because what we, as human beings experience, is perceived via the senses. There are also many ways to connect to others via the senses and ways to connect to God. Intimacy is an experience we have and can perceive by the senses. If we are to understand what we experience to be intimacy, we need to understand its sensual perception.

Sensory perception and the human experience

Beloved

Let him kiss me with the kisses of his mouth—
for your love is more delightful than wine.
Pleasing is the fragrance of your perfumes;
your name is like perfume poured out.
No wonder the maidens love you!
Take me away with you—let us hurry!
Let the king bring me into his chambers.

Friends

We rejoice and delight in you;
we will praise your love more than wine.
(1:2-4)

(Related Bible references: 1 Corinthians 12:1-31, Psalm 133:1, John 17:23, Ephesians 4:1-32, Colossians 3:14, Luke 17:20-21, John 4:24, Ephesians 5:25-32, Isaiah 49:18, Isaiah 61:10, Isaiah 62:5, Jeremiah 2:2, Hosea 3:1, 1 Corinthians 13:4-6, Genesis 3:6-7, Exodus 34:6, Psalm 71:22, Psalm 98:3)

The beautiful imagery in the Song of Solomon describes to us how those who love one another are to interact.

Society has sanitized, deodorized, and attempted to hide human relationships from the dawn of time. We have treated attraction as if it is something unnatural, something to be halted. The most basic of God-given instincts has been reduced to something demonic and evil...and yet the Song of Solomon presents the reality that such an attitude must stop.

Physical contact is an essential part of the human condition. Numerous studies have resounded to the benefits of physical touch and contact in the lives of people. People who never experience the physical contact of others eventually die. Have we ever stopped to consider why this is? It is because we, as human beings, long for intimate contact with one another.

I have met many people who insist that all they need in their lives is God. They say, "If all I have is God, then I have enough." While I believe this is true in a spiritual sense, they are trying to guard themselves against intimacy with others in this statement. In a generalized sense, it is true that God is our primary need and, that as long as we have God in our lives, we will make it. We can survive without acclamation and praise. We can live on our own, whether temporary or long-term, as we are graced to do so. We don't need to be married or have children to be successful. We don't need to have a permanent mate in our lives to be happy. Not everyone reading this will be called to be married or in a long-term relationship, as is the example root in the Song of Solomon. Everyone is, however, created for intimacy. We long for human connection because we long for intimacy. God has not created us to be an island, and especially in the Body of Christ – which is the imagery used to describe God's church (1 Corinthians 12:1-31) – we are called to interact, love, and connect to one another. God calls us to delight in one another in fellowship, love, and yes, even intimacy! We cannot ignore this fact because God has created people to dwell together in His unity (Psalm 133:1, John 17:23, Ephesians 4:1-32, Colossians 3:14).

In the modern church, we talk a lot about unity – wanting it, achieving it, and hoping for it – and yet we are uncomfortable with the most basic aspects of unity that occur between human beings. Every dynamic between the man and woman in the Song of Solomon reflects unity, which, thereby, reflects intimacy. Their speech of kisses more pleasant than wine shows pleasure in unity. When two people kiss intimately, they become one. Any way a body connects – kissing, hand holding, hugging, or greater physical contact – represents a union of intimacy. People do not, as a rule, have physical contact with people they do not like or who make them uncomfortable. This is the reason why intimate violations are so serious, and so deeply affect the human person.

We also need to note the relevance of presence in intimacy. The variety of senses described here: touch (kissing/embracing), scent (fragrance), hearing (the name poured out), sight (seeing the lover as desirable by others), and speech (speaking words of encouragement and beauty to one another) shows us that intimacy reaches us in this world, transcending time and space in experience. Intimacy introduces another aspect to our being, because of its all-encompassing transcendence: the spiritual sense, or the perception of God in our midst. When Jesus told us that the Kingdom of God is within us (Luke 17:20-21), He was reminding us of an intimate principle with God and one another. God is Spirit (John 4:24), and He is perpetually with us. While He does not live in this world, He is as near to us and with us as our next breath. God is forever with us, as is His Kingdom, His eternal reign. The Kingdom of God has always existed, and always will exist. So too, as the Kingdom of God is within us, that Greek word also means, by extension, "among and around." The Kingdom of God is within us as God lives in us, His temples of the Holy Spirit – among us, as we live by His principles and in His love, and among us, as we recognize His intimate presence with us and we respond in kind to it, aware that He is wherever His people are.

The intimate presence of God, in transcending the senses, also reminds of us of the experience that we can have with God perceived by our senses. Many within the modern church have found reasons to make the senses or sensual experience (as experience by the senses) evil or carnal rather than existential. Sex and sexual experience have been classified as "sensual" because it incorporates so many different senses into its experience. This does not limit sex to the only experience in our lives that relates experience by senses. One of the primary reasons the Song of Solomon incorporates the extent of sexual descriptiveness within its pages is because of its power to illicit an understanding of transcendent intimacy with both the senses and the supernatural. Our experience with God is also an experience that we can have by our senses. While we know we cannot rely on our senses alone in our relationship with God, we also cannot deny the realization of His presence by the senses. People can debate and argue about the existence of God all day long and have done so for centuries. We can make the presence of God words on a page – and, therefore, debatable – or we can recognize that perceiving and experiencing God by the senses makes our encounter with God something real, something tangible, and yet ethereal. It lets us know of God's presence beyond a theological or philosophical musing, moving into the realm of the existential. God becomes, therefore, present within our realm of understanding and experience. If we consider God's creation, spiritual gifts, rituals, and rites to us, our experience with God can be felt and experienced within all five of our senses: touch (healing, laying on of hands, anointing, service, mercy, giving); hearing (prophecy, interpreting tongues, word of wisdom, word of knowledge, encouragement, teaching); speech (teaching, speaking in tongues, word of wisdom, word of knowledge, prophecy); taste (communion, experiencing God's bounty); smell (the aroma of the Lord as manifest through His creation); and sight (discernment of spirits, miraculous wonders, visions and dreams). Groups that attempt to deny these essential experiences with God by which we know God is real in a way that we cannot be argued or debated are missing out on a very important experience: the very presence of God while we live in this world in the Kingdom of God this side of heaven.

I have long taught that marriage is a type of the relationship destined to exist between Christ and the church (Ephesians 5:25-32). All throughout the Bible, God's relationship imagery is a marriage between Him and His people (Isaiah 49:18, Isaiah 61:10, Isaiah 62:5, Jeremiah 2:2, Hosea 3:1). This imagery is used, as it is used here in the Song of Solomon, as a description of intimacy. God provides for His people in trust, in an unspoken dynamic of love. He constantly provides in His provision for them, calling us, speaking to us, and watching and waiting as His people respond in kind through their love and adoration. Intimacy indicates and demands relationship: marriage, friendship, family, camaraderie, support, and most of all, love. Thus, the Song of Solomon pictures intimate relationships and aspects therein, calling us to pay attention to our human relationships as much as our heavenly relationships – because one powerfully reflects the other.

Verses 2-4 emphasize a sense of gratitude for relationship based in intimacy. The partners are grateful for one another. They realize that the relationship they have one to another is unique. That realization comes from their intimate connection. Through intimacy, they know they have something that they don't have with someone else.

Intimacy is intimidating this side of heaven and can also be disconcerting at times if we are not where we need to be with the Lord. Even if we are where we need to be with God, intimate interaction can have its complications and difficulties. It's overwhelming to realize the level of exposure we have when dealing with others in an intimate dynamic. Having someone who knows and loves us so intimately can cause us to withdraw. This is why love with intimacy is so powerful. If we consider 1 Corinthians 13 and the different things it says about love, we find those things within the balances of intimacy: patience, kindness, non-envious, not boastful, not proud, not dishonoring, not self-seeking, not easily angered, not keeping a record of wrongs, not delighting in evil, rejoicing in the truth, always protecting, trusting, hoping, and persevering (1 Corinthians 13:4-6). These amazing qualities are seen in intimate contact, made real – manifesting in human beings, mere flesh – as they can interact with one another in an intimate way.

1 Corinthians 13 often contains verses that seem intangible and unobtainable in this world, because without a sensory visual of them, we do not perceive them to be real. Unfortunately, many people skip over these dynamics in favor of use and abuse. One of the first things that happened during the fall of mankind was a profound sense of loss in intimate dynamics between Adam and Eve. Now aware of nakedness, they clothed themselves before one another. Innocence was replaced by shrewdness, suspicious behavior, and judgments (Genesis 3:6-7). Down the line many years later, we find the same complications in intimate relationships today. Due to the sinfulness of others, intimacy is often violated, or one lives in fear of that violation.

The only way such fear and violation are overcome is through intimacy – and making intimacy an experience one can perceive and know for themselves. The answer is not to talk about something distant and intangible. Living in the natural means we deal with issues that compromise intimacy – broken trust, infidelity, abuse, and heartache. Some people in this world hurt so deeply and so intimately that they find it difficult to trust an intimate partner. In intimacy, there should be trust. Restoring intimacy comes about the creation of this experience through love. A good intimate partner is patient with the difficulties and recognizes intimate trust is earned, not forced. Over time, we should all be aware of what we have in our relationships, especially when they are solid in intimacy, no matter how that manifests. Clearly the lover and the beloved in the Song of Solomon were keenly aware of the awesome 'catch' they had in one another. They were aware that their physical attributes, their charm, their personalities, and the essence of who they were would be, at times, attractive to others. In intimacy, they trusted one another to maintain the private aspects of their intimate dynamic. The same is true for us today. When we experience intimacy, we should be grateful and recognize what we have in that, be the intimacy in a good friend, a good husband or wife, a good boyfriend or girlfriend, a good leader, a good family member, or even just someone that we can trust. We can see in that individual all the essential qualities that make them desirable to others and express a sense of gratitude for the fact that they are our friend – husband – wife – parent – leader – or other intimate relationship – and recognize God working within them as a blessing.

The other end of receiving intimacy is giving it, as well. Those with whom we are most intimate should know what they mean to us. We should express our gratitude in kind, extending toward them the love they extend to us. It's great to know that we can trust others. In a world that proves itself untrustworthy, we must cleave even more to trustworthy, faithful, intimate people in our lives. Love is not just shown in words, in sex, or in some sort of grand gesture, but in the ability to be faithful with others. At the end of the day, that faithfulness we find in intimacy will matter more than all the hurts and wounds we might have experienced elsewhere. Love in intimacy is a giving and a receiving, that transforms thoughts and perspectives to bring us to a purposed place of balance.

All this points us back to our relationship with God in a big way. Those faithful, intimate people in our lives remind us of the fidelity, love, and faithfulness of our God. Just like false people fail us, so too, false gods fail us.

Seeing the things we chased after in our lives, often with a haste and intimacy, reminds us of the greatness of God. Where these false things led us astray and hurt us, God has never failed us (Exodus 34:6, Psalm 71:22, Psalm 98:3)! He loved us where we were, with our flaws and issues, and restored us to where we needed to be. Now we dwell in communion with Him, in a profound sense of intimacy, where we know that He loves us, and we too, love Him. Eternity is not enough time to herald the praises of the God we know and serve!

We also see a key of excitement and haste. When people dwell in intimacy, they desire to be together. There is an urgency to meet with a friend, family member, or beloved when something happens, good or bad. The desire to share important and special things – even personal things – with one another exists. Friends desire to talk and spend time together. Lovers desire to be together, share things together, and delve into a more private, physical relationship that is shared exclusively by the two. A child desires to sit in its parent's lap and hear a story, sit and talk, or sometimes just sit and be held. Intimacy craves contact and there is an excitement to sit and dwell in that place of security.

If there is someone in your life (regardless of their "title" in relationship to you) and you dread their presence or do not seek to be with them in excitement, it is indicative of a problem in the intimate dynamic. As was said earlier, intimacy either exists, or it does not. We cannot force other people to share a sense of intimacy or force an intimate relationship to exist at whim. If we don't feel right about a relationship, it is, most likely, not right for us. Experiences of intimacy are different for different people and different relationships express the dynamics of intimacy differently. If we dread being with someone, their intimate dynamics do not align with ours. There is no sin in this realization. The only thing that is wrong when one has this realization is to try and pursue a dynamic that is not there.

In contrast, we should always be excited – go with fervor and haste – to the place where we can be with God, our Father. Worship, praise, hearing the spoken Word, learning from or reading the Scriptures, and doing His work should always be something we look forward to with pursuit and excitement. We cannot spend enough time with God, learning from God, or gleaning from God, because our ultimate longing should be to become united deeper with our heavenly Father. The more time we spend with Him, the greater our preparation in pursuit of eternity.

Do we delight in one another? Do we delight in God? Do we enjoy, take pleasure in, and experience the mutual blessing of love and care God has placed us here to give and receive? It is time to examine this and examine ourselves as we delve deeper into the purposed human desire for intimacy.

Sensory perception and our royal spiritual heritage

Lover

*I liken you, my darling, to a mare
harnessed to one of the chariots of Pharaoh.
Your cheeks are beautiful with earrings,
your neck with strings of jewels.
We will make you earrings of gold,
studded with silver.*

Beloved

*While the king was at his table,
my perfume spread its fragrance.
My lover is to me a sachet of myrrh
resting between my breasts.
My lover is to me a cluster of henna blossoms
from the vineyards of En Gedi.*

Lover

How beautiful you are, my darling!
Oh, how beautiful!
Your eyes are doves.
(1:9-15)

(Related Bible references: Matthew 20:28, Mark 10:45, Luke 22:6, John 12:26, Romans 12:7, Galatians 5:13, 1 Peter 4:10, 1 Peter 3:3-4, 1 Peter 2:4-10, Genesis 8:21, Leviticus 4:7, Ezekiel 20:28, 2 Corinthians 2:15, Ephesians 5:2, Philippians 4:18, Matthew 6:22, Luke 11:34, Matthew 3:16, Mark 1:10, Luke 3:22, John 1:32)

The imagery in chapter 1 verses 9-15 relates to royalty. Both the lover and the beloved speak in terms of having the best and most powerful through royal imagery. Today if you compared a woman to a horse, she would most likely see it as an insult. She would hear herself being compared to an animal and perceived as being fat, unruly, or maybe even stubborn. Given the context of the Song of Solomon, however, this is truly not the case. In ancient times, horses were considered prized animals. They were used for transportation, battle, and as a sign of royalty. How many horses someone had was as much an indication of wealth as how much they had of something else. The mare was considered prized because it could also generate a profit by bearing young.

The specific imagery provided in verse 9 is of a mare harnessed to Pharaoh's chariot. This tells us a lot about the way the man viewed this woman. He saw her fit to serve the king, agile, swift, solid, strong, and prized. Only the best of the best was fit to serve the king's chariot. This means within her – despite any flaws she may have had – her beloved saw her as perfect and without flaw or defect.

In both the practical and spiritual realms, God has appointed us as "fit to serve." We know, as Christians, that we are called to service for one another (Matthew 20:28, Mark 10:45, Luke 22:6, John 12:26, Romans 12:7, Galatians 5:13, 1 Peter 4:10). We also know that, in Christ,

God sees us in Him, without spot or blemish. The practical side of this for our relationships with one another is simple: those we involve ourselves with on an intimate level need to see and understand our worth and value. The people to whom we are closest can help launch us into destiny, or they can help keep us down. Not only did he see her empowered, but he also recognized her worth and fitness to serve royalty. The same is true with us today. Our intimate companions need to see our worth, value, and recognize our fitness to serve the King. They cannot see us as their personal servants or as people to be used and abused, but by prized servants of the ultimate King of Kings. Understanding the prized worth and value worthy of royalty changes the perception of an individual in a relationship. If everyone could perceive themselves as God views them, keeping the royal view of eternal purpose in mind, the way we interact in intimate relationships would be very different.

We also can see the incredible adornment in precious jewels and metals as an enhancement of royal beauty. While some claiming to be Christian believe wearing jewelry or cosmetics is sinful, the Bible uses jewelry and cosmetics alike as both an enhancement of beauty and a symbolism of royalty, prohibiting neither for the Christian believer. It is true the Bible advises us to focus on inward things rather than on those exterior (1 Peter 3:3-4), but if we take the Bible in true context, it does not prohibit us from wearing jewelry or using cosmetics. If anything, jewelry and cosmetics are a powerful and symbolic reminder of our royal heritage in Jesus Christ (1 Peter 2:4-10).

The royal imagery continues, speaking of the king's presence at his table. The fragrance of the woman travels to the king's table, making her presence known. This proves the power of sensual experience and sensation within the human experience. They go on to describe the lover as a sachet of myrrh and a cluster of blossoms – both which also give off fragrance. While physical adornment brings pleasure to sight, fragrance brings pleasure to the sense of smell. Studies have shown the powerful role scent ties in with memory. The illustration and use of senses so intricately in the Song of Solomon explains to us another foundational basis for experiencing God and the world through our senses. Senses bring essential things, memories, precepts, and teachings to mind, and using them in the spiritual serves as a divine "mnemonic device" of sorts. Throughout the Old Testament, the Scriptures spoke of the burnt offerings as a "sweet savor" or "fragrance to the Lord" (Genesis 8:21, Leviticus 4:7, Ezekiel 20:28). The fragrance of the offerings was a sweet, beautiful fragrance because the forgiveness of sin was associated with that scent (2 Corinthians 2:15, Ephesians 5:2, Philippians 4:18). In relationships, a lover remembers their mate's perfume or cologne, the scent of their skin, the taste of their lips, the touch of their skin, their touch, the sound of their voice. All these sensual reminders are reminders of the love and the relationship shared between the two: maybe a special gift, a special encounter, a romantic experience, a special day, and so on and so forth. The sensual experience we have with God is designed to instill the same type of memory within us: it is to remind us this side of heaven that God has forgiven our sins, He still forgives our sins and wants to have a place and presence within our everyday lives. God is not distant, but is as near as our next sensual experience that reminds us He is with us in everything we go through. All we must do is reach out to Him to experience His presence in our lives.

Lastly, the lover compares the beloved's eyes to doves. We know from the New Testament that the eyes are the light of the body (Matthew 6:22, Luke 11:34) and a dove represents the Holy Spirit of God (Matthew 3:16, Mark 1:10, Luke 3:22, John 1:32). Within the beauty of this woman, the lover saw God's presence. He saw the Holy Spirit working through and within her, recognizing God as her Creator. In the faces, the eyes, and the lives of those we know, we need to see the presence of God and the work of God. Those we love do not belong to us in a possessive sense; they belong to God. Seeing God at work in them reminds us even more of how much we need to embrace God in our lives and respect His work in others.

Intimate experience

Your lips drop sweetness as the honeycomb, my bride;
milk and honey are under your tongue.
The fragrance of your garments is like that of Lebanon.
You are a garden locked up, my sister, my bride;
you are a spring enclosed, a sealed fountain.
Your plants are an orchard of pomegranates
with choice fruits,
with henna and nard,
nard and saffron,
calamus and cinnamon,
with every kind of incense tree,
with myrrh and aloes
and all the finest spices.
You are a garden fountain,
a well of flowing water
streaming down from Lebanon.

Beloved

Awake, north wind,
and come, south wind!
Blow on my garden,
that its fragrance may spread abroad.
Let my lover come into his garden
and taste its choice fruits.
I have come into my garden, my sister, my bride;
I have gathered my myrrh with my spice.
I have eaten my honeycomb and my honey;
I have drunk my wine and my milk.

Friends

Eat, O friends, and drink;
drink your fill, O lovers.
(Song of Solomon 4:11-5:1)

Friends

Who is this that appears like the dawn,
fair as the moon, bright as the sun,
majestic as the stars in procession?

Lover

I went down to the grove of nut trees
to look at the new growth in the valley,
to see if the vines had budded
or the pomegranates were in bloom.
Before I realized it,
my desire set me among the royal chariots
of my people.

Friends

Come back, come back, O Shulammite;
come back, come back, that we may gaze on you!
Why would you gaze on the Shulammite
as on the dance of Mahanaim?
(6:10-13)

(Related Bible References: Genesis 2:7)

Now that we have looked at the sensory experience and its role in intimacy, I want to investigate the experience of intimacy itself. We have looked at the sensory role in intimacy because intimacy is perceived by the senses in the natural realm. It is something we experience via taste, touch, sound, sight, and smell. Intimacy, however, does not just begin and end with sensual experience – it also exists by the Spirit.

How do we define a spiritual experience? Most of them we try to define by our senses or our emotions. Explaining any sort of experience can be a difficult task, because what we experience, we perceive through our own perceptions. In the verses above, the man and woman seek to describe more than just the way they feel about one another; they are describing a feeling, an experience that they have with one another. It comes out personified, as a result. Trying to describe intimacy requires us to compare it to something else – and what we often compare it to are things that we, once again perceive by the senses.

I've been asked to describe the experience of intimacy. In trying to write this book, this was a particular section I stumbled over. Instead of trying to figure it out on my own, I took a Facebook poll to gather a list of people's favorite love songs. Some of the choices were *All of Me* by John Legend, *Unconditionally* by Katy Perry, *The Woman in Me (Needs The Man in You)* by Shania Twain, *The Power of Love* by Celine Dion, *Truly, Madly, Deeply* by Savage Garden, *How Do You Talk to an Angel?* by the Heights, *Something* by the Beatles, *Crazy Love* by Van Morrison, *Here and Now* by Luther Vandross, *Chasing Cars* by Snow Patrol, and *Everything I Do (I Do for You)* by Bryan Adams. Every one of these songs expresses a level of intimacy, from the initial stages of meeting and knowing, to a deeper love that transcends time.

I believe the perception of intimacy is dependent upon the experience of the individual. Some people are stronger in one sensory area than another, and some people are more spiritually aware than others. That is why history is full of different intimate expressions, including songs, painting, sculptures, and various writings. In kind, people prefer or touch on different expressions of intimacy in their own experiences. There is no right or wrong answer in the expression of intimacy; none is superior over another. Some display a certain awkwardness in the beginning of intimate expressions, while others move to a place of ease and grace in the true beauty and flow found therein between two people in an intimate dynamic.

If I were to pick one song that resonates with me as to the expression of intimacy, it is *Breathe* by Faith Hill. This is because in my own experience, I describe intimacy as being like breathing: it is something I started doing one day and have not ever stopped since. It's never away from me, no matter where I go. I can't see it in the natural, but I can perceive it by the Spirit. It is as necessary for life as the move of the air and the breath of life. You know it is there, even as you go about your daily life, and its presence around you is a constant reminder that there is someone out there who you have something with that transcends time and space. Intimacy lets you know of a love that exists even at a distance, simply because it surrounds, transforms, and breathes life into your very existence.

Breathing is also a good comparison for intimacy because it echoes the point that dwelling in intimacy does not require expectation. We breathe because it is a part of being; and intimate love is also a part of being. An intimate couple can just be together. One who is intimate with God can just be with God. It's not about parading the relationship in front of everyone, nor is it about what everyone else thinks. In intimacy, you just know that you are there, with your Beloved. Love surrounds, connection surrounds, and reminds us that life is greater than we are.

The comparison of intimacy to breath is important because it reminds us of the first breath of life breathed into mankind by God at creation. From that singular moment, we find the spark of life – that which gives it meaning, purpose, and creativity. The word for "breath" used in Genesis 2:7 is *neshamah*, which literally means "breath, spirit."[16] It refers to both the Spirit of God and the spirit living in man. This tells us that the spirit which animates our life comes from God, and is a powerful connection between us and God, and us and other human beings. Our very breath is a reminder of soul and spirit, of something that connects us to God from the very beginning. From that first moment of true intimacy between God and humanity, we find a key purpose of intimacy: life. Intimacy is a life-force that envelops, encompasses, surrounds, and is ever-with us. Intimacy has a purpose, and that purpose is life, as we find a unity of people together, and people with God. As the result of intimacy, life comes forth: natural, physical, spiritual, and an extension of the spiritual, creativity. Intimacy inspires us; it inspires us to live, just knowing that connection exists that transcends something in the natural. Intimacy proves life is more than what we may muse intellectually. It is also a sensory and spiritual experience that has profound meaning as we pursue intimacy in trust in our lives. If we deny that experience, we are denying a primary way we experience intimacy, and come into a place where we find the deeper discovery of God at work within, through, among, and around us.

As long as we are alive, we will continue to have experiences that we can perceive by the senses. Intimacy is one such experience. The more we are in touch with what we perceive via the senses, the more in touch we will be with the presence of God around us. This will lead us to greater intimacy with Him – and greater intimacy with others.

CHAPTER 5

The Challenge

Key verses

- **Verses 8:3-4:** *His left arm is under my head and his right arm embraces me. Daughters of Jerusalem, I charge you: Do not arouse or awaken love until it so desires.*

- **Verses 8:6-7:** *Place me like a seal over your heart, like a seal on your arm; for love is as strong as death, its jealousy unyielding as the grave. It burns like blazing fire, like a mighty flame. Many waters cannot quench love; rivers cannot wash it away. If one were to give all the wealth of his house for love, it would be utterly scorned.*

Words and phrases to know

- **Brother:** From the Hebrew word *'achl* which means "brother"[1]

- **Despise:** From the Hebrew word *buwz* which means "to despise, hold in contempt, hold as insignificant."[2]

- **Embrace:** From the Hebrew word *chabaq* which means "to embrace, clasp."[3]

- **Seal:** From the Hebrew word *chowtham* which means "seal, signet, signet ring."[4]

- **Death:** From the Hebrew word *maveth* which means "death, dying, Death (personified), realm of the dead."[5]

- **Jealousy:** From the Hebrew word *qin'ah* which means "ardour, zeal, jealousy."[6]

- **Voice:** From the Hebrew word *qowl* which means "voice, sound, noise; lightness, frivolity."[7]

If only you were to me like a brother,
who was nursed at my mother's breasts!
Then, if I found you outside,
I would kiss you,
and no one would despise me.
I would lead you
and bring you to my mother's house—
she who has taught me.
I would give you spiced wine to drink,
the nectar of my pomegranates.
His left arm is under my head
and his right arm embraces me.
Daughters of Jerusalem, I charge you:
Do not arouse or awaken love
until it so desires.
(8:1-4)

(Related Bible references: Revelation 7:17, 21:4, 1 Corinthians 6;19)

W hen I started this study in the Song of Solomon, it challenged me. It was an initial challenge because of its prose and style of writing. It didn't fit in the same format as prior commentaries I have done. It wasn't easy to write about because it was so repetitive. Then, as I got more into the commentary, it challenged me on an entirely different level: the content addressed many aspects of intimacy, of life, and of relationships that I was not prepared to confront personally. As I have gone through this study, I have been challenged on all levels: in my writing, personally, and spiritually. Studying the Song of Solomon has truly changed my own perceptions of what I believed intimacy to be, how it functioned, and what to look for when identifying it.

I didn't expect the challenge that I found in this book, because I've never been so challenged by a writing before. Never have I attempted to tackle such complex themes – with further complex undertones – in one writing. The Song of Solomon addresses so many different facets of human life: men and women, attraction, relationships, desire, sex, sexism, patriarchy, spirituality, and beauty. Within its pages, we find some of the deepest thoughts on life, all written through the eyes of a few people who love one another and desire to celebrate the special and unique connection they have together.

What I realize as I review the pages of this writing is that the Song of Solomon poses a challenge for all of us, because the very content of this book pertains to the essence of life and the discovery of purpose therein. That challenge is to trust God and take the plunge into intimacy when it finds us – there, we will find life. I believe that, at some point in time, most people will come into a place where intimacy will find them. The Song of Solomon makes us realize it is not something to be feared. So many people go through life with a fear of intimacy that blocks them from coming head-to-head with it in a way that it will change their lives. This is not God's will for our lives. Intimacy is something to be lived. There's a reason romantic and erotic novels, romantic comedies, erotica, love stories, love songs, buddy shows and movies, and even friendship movies are so universally popular: they tap into something within each person that desires to connect to someone else. Every one of us wants to have someone who we feel about and long for, and who feels the way that we do, in kind. We seek the excitement, the passion, and the love, just as is described in the verses of chapter 8 above. We long to have friends to talk to, share life with, and celebrate the seasons of our lives. We want it all: intimacy on all its levels. Despite the fears, the walls, and the personal barriers we build to avoid intimacy, it is something we all long for. The Song of Solomon taps into this desire and challenges us to pursue it – believe for it and in it – live it.

God doesn't desire us to go through life with mediocre relationships and mediocre connections to others. So many of us settle for mediocre for so many reasons: to please their parents or other family members, to settle down because one has reached a certain age, because we feel pressured into a relationship by others (or maybe even the church) around us, or just because it's something we think we must do. Some pursue the mediocre because they themselves have been hurt, abused, or mistreated in another relationship – thus, they fear intimacy will hurt them, too. In this most profound writing, the Song of Solomon encourages us to receive intimacy for ourselves. No matter how hurt we have been, intimacy can serve as a place of sanctuary in our lives. A sanctuary is a place of safety, a holy place, one set apart by God for His purposes. In intimacy, we come to find the most pleasant, the most pleasing, and the most desirable of things we can obtain. Relationships hold no true power to heal without intimacy, as deep wounds heal only by deep love. While it is wonderful to know God loves us and feel His love in our lives, it is also a healing balm to see His love working in an intimate partner. It is a type, a shadow of what is to come when every tear will be wiped away and the pain of former things are remembered no more (Revelation 7:17, Revelation 21:4). In intimate relationships, the past hurts and wounds of former relationships and pains seems dimmer, further away, more of a distant reality that it seems to be in its active state. A good relationship by its own upholding can heal the hardest heart, the deepest wound...just by two people walking so intimately, they truly stand to heal the other's heart.

In the same way, God does not just want us to accept a mediocre relationship with Him, either. The important type present in intimate relationships points us to the greater reality, which is His work of wholeness within us. The Scriptures tell us God is Father, Friend, Husband, Provider, Healer, Savior, Deliverer, Victory, Sustainer, Governor, and beyond. He is so much more than we can express in the limitations of language. The things you learned about God growing up, in traditional religion and Sunday school, may or may not be an accurate representation of God. Most likely, what you have received consists of some truths and some inaccuracies about Who He is and what He desires for you and to see in you. We need not be afraid to approach God. Just as the lovers in the Song of Solomon are drawn to one another and desire to be in each other's presence, God longs for this with us. It is a pleasing place, one that brings a certain state of sanctuary within each one of us. We will encounter storms in this life; we are living in this world. We will encounter trials; we do not live in this world by ourselves. No matter what we are going through as we pass through this life, we can reach out to God, to dwell in His presence as temples of the Holy Spirit (1 Corinthians 6:19). He will stay with us, hold us, embrace us, shelter us, and bring us the best He has for us as we rejoice with Him in the times of blessing, and hold fast in the times of trial. He is the Lover of our soul; the One Who loves us beyond anything we can conceive. We get a picture of this intimacy as we pursue it for ourselves with another person – but we experience the full presence of it as we pursue it with God.

The challenge to our relationships

Place me like a seal over your heart,
like a seal on your arm;
for love is as strong as death,
its jealousy unyielding as the grave.
It burns like blazing fire,
like a mighty flame.
Many waters cannot quench love;
rivers cannot wash it away.
If one were to give
all the wealth of his house for love,
it would be utterly scorned.
(8:6-7)

(Related Bible references: Ephesians 5:22-33, Matthew 19:6, Mark 10:9, Ezekiel 23:37, Revelation 17:2, Revelation 18:3, Jeremiah 3:6-9, Hosea 4:15, John 3:16-18, John 7:24)

Just like the Song of Solomon challenges us to accept intimacy in our lives, so too do intimate relationships challenge us to be, give, and receive more than we ever have before. As we discussed earlier, so much of what we perceive a good relationship to be lies in social notions about traditional relationships. The Song of Solomon is here to make us look far beyond what we think defines a good relationship and stop reducing people to roles and policies. If God desires the best for us as people, attempting to define successful relationships by narrowly defined concepts of roles and rituals is a mistake. If God desires us to discover intimacy with Him and with one another, we need to allow intimacy to change us, and our hardened concepts about what makes a relationship work.

We push and pull so much today for a defense of what we call "traditional marriage." We want our relationships to look like a 1950s cereal commercial instead of like the type God has commissioned us to be. Intimacy doesn't exist in roles and stereotypes! A good relationship is not about having two and a half children in tow and living in a sprawling mansion. Intimacy is the truest definition of relationship between godly partners whom God has fitly joined together. It is obvious that in pursuit of something other than God's purposes for our relationship, intimacy does not exist in many of these "traditional" marriages. That is why divorce rates are high and so many marriages are unhappy. Staying in situations without true intimacy leads to unhappiness and unfaithfulness which leads to a deep void in one's life. When a situation for true intimacy arises, it causes conflict.

If we want our relationships to be better, we need to stop upholding worldly concepts of relationship dynamics and start seeking God about true intimacy and where it can be found in our lives. We also need to understand different types of intimacy that exist between people and ways intimacy can help us develop stronger bonds as people. This means we need to stop judging by mere appearances and legalities and make a right judgment (John 7:24)! We need to step back and recognize the power of intimacy and its driving force in what defines relationship in the Spiritual realm rather than just the legal or governmental arenas we see today. What makes people in a relationship? What makes people married? What makes them divorced? Is it the simple act of signing a document, or is it something more? What is God's will for relationship partners? What is the purpose in relationship to begin with?

The intimate relationship between men and women is a type of the relationship between Christ and the Church, which I have already stated (Ephesians 5:22-33). This bond of intimacy is described as love. Both partners sacrifice something within themselves to give to the other, while receiving something more desirable, perfect, and purposeful back. They don't become a different person in the sense that their tastes, hopes, and individual personhood changes – but they become a person they did not know they could become. This person that each partner becomes as they aspire to greater connection is the true mark of a beloved. They each let the other develop in every way, without hindrance, no matter the sacrifice to self. God doesn't give up on us. In intimacy, those truly joined by God don't give up on each other, either.

Adultery, which we spoke of earlier as a barrier to intimacy, is a word we throw around a lot today. People claim someone has committed adultery if they had sex with someone who wasn't their spouse before they were ever married, to describe a relationship one has after they are divorced, and even to use as a weapon against people at times who have never even been married. The term "adultery" isn't so loose in God's definition. It is used as an image to describe the disruption of intimacy in a relationship. The definition, however, has certain limits. It is speaking of God's view of an intimate relationship, not man's concept of what defines a relationship. The Bible says what God has put together should remain...it says nothing about the numerous relationships we create and hope He will put His seal of approval upon (Matthew 19:6, Mark 10:9). In this same vain, adultery is also defined as idolatry (Ezekiel 23:37, Revelation 17:2, Revelation 18:3), a breaking of the covenant between God and His people (Jeremiah 3:6-9, Hosea 4:15). The Bible never describes non-believers as being guilty of committing a spiritual adultery. The reason: they did not have the kind of relationship with the Father to be classified as committing spiritual adultery. The natural type of that which is brought together by the Spirit reflects that which is spiritual in marriage. If the right relationship does not exist, it cannot rightly be called marriage, nor intimacy, and ending it cannot be classified as an idolatry or adultery. In this, we learn that the type present in a relationship cannot substitute for the reality behind it. A relationship that is not serving its purpose as a type lacks the intimacy needed to draw both partners closer to God through it. Holding onto it thus becomes an idol, and both partners commit a spiritual adultery against God as they idolize the concepts, hopes, and aspirations they had for a relationship that was not His doing.

God wants us to look at our relationships. He wants us to stop pursing that which is worldly and start pursuing intimacy, which is spiritual. Pursuing infatuation after infatuation does not lead us to intimacy. Infatuation is blind; intimate love is not. Pursuing relationships for the wrong reasons does not lead us to intimacy. If our relationships lack intimacy, we do not find the type – and the truth – that we need to discover about ourselves, about the one we love, and about our heavenly Father.

My favorite verse in the Song of Solomon is found in this section above: it states that love is stronger than death. In ancient times, death was considered the one thing that could never be overcome. No matter how much people tried to avoid it, it reared its ugly head through war, famine, infant mortality, violence, illness, and old age. To say love was stronger than death has two important meanings. The first is that love is truly something born of and from God. It is His greatest gift to us – something that overcomes everything, including death. The second meaning relates to the first – it contains the promise of the resurrection – that Christ would come and overcome death with life by love (John 3:16-18). Every one of us needs to know love is stronger than death and see it alive in our relationships as well as know it is there in our relationship with God. If there is one thing we all need, it is a touch of love to stand as a sign, a reminder, and a power that can never be overcome by any worldly or natural means.

Come away, my beloved to a place of contentment

Lover

*You who dwell in the gardens
with friends in attendance,
let me hear your voice!*

Beloved

Come away, my lover,
and be like a gazelle
or like a young stag
on the spice-laden mountains.
(8:13-14)

(Related Bible references: 1 John 4:18)

It's not uncommon to see television commercials for various internet dating sites. Some claim to be based on "scientific methods of compatibility," by which they generate your "perfect match." The people on the commercials praise the site's benefits, saying had they not used it, they would not have been so perfectly matched. What the sites do not tell you about are the many people who were perhaps dissatisfied with the site, or who wound up divorced because their methods of "scientific connection" just didn't work for them. The Song of Solomon reminds us that compatibility is more than science, more than a method of "matching" based on human understanding. The person Who ultimately matches those led by His Spirit into relationship with one another is still God, our Father, in Heaven. Yes, people can pursue relationships out of His will, but these do not bear the fruit of true intimacy where both give and receive. The experience of intimacy calls out, as each partner calls out to one another. It is, most likely, based on something that can't be explained in mere words – maybe even both those in the intimate relationship can't explain it to one another. In the day they met, God called to each, and they called out to each other, to dwell in a place of safety and beauty.

Intimacy is a reminder that science, the world we can immediately run to and rely on, and secular methods do not have the final say. There is more to the human person than checked boxes or filled-out forms. There is also more to life than the theories, hypothesis, and analysis of mankind. We are more than just beings in a fleshly body, biding time and randomly connecting at whim. Intimacy proves, once and for all, that God and spiritual things do exist. It does this without ever preaching a message, attempting to convince people about God or doctrine; it even does it without saying a word. Intimacy is a witness, a testimony all its own.

What does this mean for us? It means our relationships are important. Who we connect to is important. How we treat others – and how we allow ourselves to be treated – is important. Our relationships are a way in which we witness and reach out to others. We can stand and try to evangelize people all day long, but having solid, loving couples, friends, family members, leaders, and yes, even by extension, brothers and sisters in the church, helps us come to a greater relationship with God in our everyday lives. Intimacy with God and others gives us a sense of ourselves and God at work within us. It gives us hope – hope for ourselves, for the church, and for humanity as a whole – proving that connection in love truly does cast out all fear (1 John 4:18).

Too many today feel like they are getting nowhere with God, and with others. Too many today live in a state of despair, isolation, and fear because of wrong pursuits and wrong people in their lives. Many look for love in the wrong places or think success and love will find them if they only pursue material things. Intimacy is the answer as it breaks through the despair, loneliness, alienation, and depravation to a place where contentment can flow because one has a sense of belonging and purpose, just by being who God has created them to be.

Think this kind of love is a myth? It is not, I assure you. God is calling. He is calling His church to Him in a way where this type of love can stand fruitful, fragrant, and visible. He longs to see His people happy, contented, satisfied, and purposed in every possible way of their lives. God desires the best for us in our relationships, where we can stand in a place where it is you...your intimate

partner…and those to whom you are closest…
And, of course, your True Beloved…
Jehovah God.

CONCLUSION

When It's All Been Said and Done

Be still and know that I am God. – Psalm 46:10

The Song of Solomon ends rather abruptly. The two just stop speaking, or singing, or prosing, or...whatever it was they were specifically doing. There's no fanfare, no conclusion, no dismissal to the big post-party event – there's just the last verse. We don't hear about the rest of their lives together, about the children they had, about their first fight, or anything else about them as people. This doesn't mean they weren't people with issues, or that their relationship didn't change over time. Does the pause mean the couple faded from the forefront? Did their intimate bond end? In most books of the Bible, there seems to be some conclusion to the presented text. That's not so in the Song of Solomon. So what does this pause mean – is the pause the end?

I've been thinking the past few days as to why this is. The reason the Song of Solomon has no ending is because it's still going on. The dynamics of intimacy never end. It is an eternal song, an eternal connection, and it doesn't end with the end of a text. Intimacy is beyond words, and that means words are limited to describe the depths and power of intimate connection. As long as we interact with other people and, in the beyond, as long as we interact with God, intimacy will always exist. Thus, the Song of

Solomon continues in the bounds and dynamics of intimate connection, right down to this very day.

So, if intimacy is eternal and doesn't end, why isn't the text longer? Isn't there more to say? No, there isn't – and that is the point. The text itself ends because after a while, there are no more words to say. Intimacy is either there, or it's not. While we could go on and on about the attributes of it, what it feels like to the people, what it looks like, but in intimacy, there comes a point where all the words have been said.

Just because the words stop doesn't mean the intimacy ends. We live in a world that is generally uncomfortable with quiet. We've come to associate silence with anger and passive-aggressive behavior. We think noise, entertainment, and talking is always good. This is not always true. Sometimes talk, noise, and yes, even entertainment serve as distractions from the things we need to confront and deal with in our lives. The fact that the Song of Solomon simply ends – and silence remains – frees us from the concept that noise is good, quiet is bad, and silence should be used for anger.

No matter where you are in your experiences with intimacy, you can learn something from this silent pause. There is freedom in the ability to be silent with God, silent with others, and yes, even silent within yourself. There's something profound about the ability to be silent in this loud, bustling, and often confusing world. To just sit and know – know what you know you know – without having to prove anything to anyone – is a profound victory. It is in this ability that we find the power to change.

Intimacy is about a change of state; it changes our very being, from the inside out. In contrast with our modern world that makes relationships about the entertainment factor, it does not require constant entertainment, nor constant speech. On the contrary, intimacy is a 'calling out' from this world to something higher and deeper. It is in this deeper realization that we come to a complete wholeness, viewing God, others, and ourselves from a perspective of divine love.

This is not a change that comes about because we force it. It's tempting to read this book on intimacy – or any book on relationships, for that matter – and desire to run out and try to force changes. The work of intimacy is something that comes about all on its own, as we focus on God in our lives and start to center ourselves within His will. Instead of living life in the pursuit of a relationship or the pursuit of trying to fix a relationship we already have, our lives become about something greater than what we see in the immediate. Intimacy gives us a divine perspective on the things we see, the things that intimidate us, and the things that we cannot change without God's intervention.

Intimacy is about letting God work within us, despite what we see or cannot see. It is about being guided by His divine presence, even though we don't understand it. Here we find the ultimate letting go, the awareness of God near you as close as your next breath...and in that place...you find the truth and reality of life, love, and faith that you have always sought.

My call, therefore, in conclusion of this book, is to do the following: be still and know that He is God. Get to know God. Get to know His voice in your life, the move of His Spirit, the power of His presence – just because He is. Yes, God is an awesome God. He has given us so much we could praise Him throughout eternity for it. The purpose of our creation, however, is to discover Him in a deeper way: to see the work of God in everything in our lives, as a deep-running thread spanning our spiritual realities, our relationships, and our interactions with others. Intimacy fully recognizes, sees, and cherishes the realization of God working in ways completely beyond our comprehension. In this state, we are humbled, awed...and uniquely aware of spiritual realization all around and through each of us.

It's time to be still and see the profound revelation that shall come forth as the computer is unplugged, the books are put away, the cell phone is turned off, the television is no longer a focal point, and the pursuits and distractions of this world are hushed to a silent peace and powerful pause. Today we talk, and talk, and talk about things. We try to turn our do-it-yourself, self-help approaches to everything in our lives; but we can't self-help, do-it-yourself intimacy with God (or with anyone, for that matter). When it's all been said and done, the complications, the feeble attempts we've made to try and micromanage our existences will not have benefited any one of us in the least. Living in intimacy means being responsible as we are called to be and giving up our own attempts to try and control everything about our reality. In intimacy, we recognize God at work, transcending existence itself. This means that the ultimate reality of intimacy is God Himself. To a better life, to find a better place, to have better relationships, silence yourself to everything but Him. Stop trying to find, to fix, to understand within your own comprehensions. Realize His presence. Know Him in your life. Watch Him work. Then, and only then, will intimacy come forth. To find what you seek, you must first let go…and let God be God.

Yes indeed, where the words end, there the song continues, blooms, and develops, albeit in a different way. Here you can see God work, rather than try to analyze God by human limits. The Song of Solomon, here, develops in a way that requires no words, no earthly description; it simply is embraced and recognized for all it is. It doesn't make sense to the natural mind, and it doesn't have to. You don't have to explain it because those who recognize it sing it themselves and know how to sit in the presence of God born and bloomed in intimacy. Even though it may be indescribable, it will last into eternity; down the ages, down to you and God, and you and others. Intimacy makes God personal, and life interpersonal. The longer we sit in that presence, needing no explanation, the longer we will watch ourselves grow and develop because we find ourselves in the center of His will.

Be still and know that He is God. Be still and listen, watch, and learn. Most of all, be still and receive the revelation of intimacy that only the Father can give if you stop striving to make intimacy work without Him.

REFERENCES

[1] "Faith Hill Lyrics: Breathe"
http://www.azlyrics.com/lyrics/faithhill/breathe.html.
Accessed on October 21, 2013.

Introduction References

"Song Of Songs."
http://en.wikipedia.org/wiki/Song_of_Songs. Accessed on
June 26, 2012.
"Solomon." http://en.wikipedia.org/wiki/Solomon.
Accessed on June 26, 2012.

Chapter 1

[1] Strong's Exhaustive Concordance of the Bible, #7892
[2] Ibid., #4904
[3] Ibid, #1245
[4] Ibid., #8104
[5] Ibid., #0270
[6] Ibid., #5782
[7] Ibid., #0160
[8] Ibid., #2654
[9] Ibid., #1730
[10] Ibid., #4753
[11] Ibid., #3618
[12] Ibid., #3823
[13] Ibid., #2895

Chapter 2

[1] Strong's Exhaustive Concordance of the Bible, #4428
[2] Ibid., #2315
[3] Ibid., #0157
[4] Ibid., #7838
[5] Ibid., #5000
[6] Ibid., #5844
[7] Ibid., #3303
[8] Ibid., #2261
[9] Ibid., #8289
[10] Ibid., #7799
[11] Ibid., #6010
[12] Ibid., #7799
[13] Ibid., #2336
[14] Ibid, #1730
[15] Ibid., #1121
[16] Ibid., #6966
[17] Ibid., #7776
[18] Ibid., #2254
[19] Ibid., #3754
[20] Ibid., #1323
[21] Ibid., #3389
[22] Ibid., #4057
[23] Ibid., #1323
[24] Ibid., #6726
[25] Ibid., #2470
[26] Ibid., #0160
[27] Ibid., #8535
[28] Ibid., #1249
[29] "Quotes from George Carlin."
http://www.goodreads.com/quotes/52852-here-s-all-you-have-to-know-about-men-and-women. Accessed October 31, 2013.

Chapter 3

[1] Strong's Exhaustive Concordance of the Bible, #8598

[2] Ibid., #3427
[3] Ibid., #6738
[4] Ibid., #6529
[5] Ibid., #4966
[6] Ibid., #3196
[7] Ibid., #1004
[8] Ibid., #1714
[9] Ibid., #0160
[10] Ibid., #2263
[11] Ibid., #5638
[12] Ibid., #1653
[13] Ibid., #5339
[14] Ibid., #6256
[15] Ibid., #2158
[16] Ibid., #6963
[17] Ibid., #8449
[18] Ibid., #1612
[19] Ibid., #5563
[20] Ibid., #1568
[21] Ibid., #4026
[22] Ibid., #1732
[23] Ibid, #2022
[24] Ibid, #4753
[25] Ibid., #1389
[26] Ibid., #3828
[27] Ibid., #3971
[28] Ibid., #1713
[29] Ibid., #3844
[30] Ibid., #7453
[31] Ibid., #8669
[32] Ibid., #1736
[33] Ibid., #5782

Chapter 4

[1] <u>Strong's Exhaustive Concordance of the Bible</u>, #5401
[2] Ibid., #7381
[3] Ibid., #8081

[4] Ibid., #5959
[5] Ibid., #2315
[6] Ibid., #7474
[7] Ibid., #5317
[8] Ibid., #8008
[9] Ibid., #0269
[10] Ibid., #3618
[11] Ibid., #1588
[12] Ibid., #4325
[13] Ibid., #7759
[14] Ibid., #2372
[15] Ibid., #4264
[16] Ibid., #5397

Chapter 5

[1] Strong's Exhaustive Concordance of the Bible, #0251
[2] Ibid., #0936
[3] Ibid., #2263
[4] Ibid., #2368
[5] Ibid, #4194
[6] Ibid., #7068
[7] Ibid., #6963

ABOUT THE AUTHOR

Dr. Lee Ann B. Marino

Be still and know that I am God. – Psalm 46:10

Dr. Lee Ann B. Marino, Ph.D., D.Min., D.D. (she/her) is "everyone's favorite theologian" leading Gen X, Millennials, and Gen Z with expertise in leadership training, queer and feminist theology, general religion, and apostolic theology. She has served in ministry since 1998 and was ordained as a pastor in 2002 and an apostle in 2010. She founded what is now Sanctuary Apostolic Fellowship Empowerment (SAFE) Ministries in 2004. Under her ministry heading Dr. Marino is founder and Overseer of Sanctuary International Fellowship Tabernacle (SIFT) (the original home of National Coming Out Sunday) and The Sanctuary Network, and Chancellor of Apostolic Covenant Theological Seminary (ACTS).

Affectionately nicknamed "the Spitfire," Dr. Marino has spent over two decades as an "apostle, preacher, and teacher" (2 Timothy 1:11), exercising her personal mandate to become "all things to all people" (1 Corinthians 9:22). Her embrace of spiritual issues (both technical and intimate) has found its home among both seekers and believers, those who desire spiritual answers to today's issues.

Dr. Marino has preached throughout the United States, Puerto Rico, and Europe in hundreds of religious services and experiences throughout the years. A history maker in her own right, she has spent over two decades in advocacy, education, and work for and within minority spiritual communities (including African American, Hispanic, and LGBTQ+). She has also served as the first woman on all-male synods, councils, and panels, as well as the first preacher or speaker welcomed of a different race, sexual orientation, or identity among diverse communities. Today, Dr. Marino's work extends to over 150 countries as she hosts the popular *Kingdom Now* podcast, which is in the top 20 percentile of all podcasts worldwide. She is also the author of over 35 books and the popular Patheos column, *Leadership on Fire*. To date, she has had five bestselling titles within their subject matter: *Understanding Demonology, Spiritual Warfare, Healing, and Deliverance: A Manual for the Christian Minister*; *Ministry School Boot Camp: Training for Helps Ministries, Appointments, and Beyond*; *Discovering Intimacy: A Journey Through the Song of Solomon*; *Fruit of the Vine: Study and Commentary on the Fruit of the Spirit*; and *Ministering to LGBTQ+ (and Those Who Love Them): A Primer for Queer Theology* (and its accompanying workbook).

As a public icon and social media influencer, Dr. Marino advocates healthy body image (curvy/full-figured), representation as a demisexual/aromantic, and albinism awareness as a model. Known to those she works with, she is a spiritual mom, teacher, leader, professor, confidant, and friend. She continues to transform, receiving new teaching, revelation, and insight in this thing we call "ministry." Through years of spiritual growth and maturity, Dr. Marino stands as herself, here to present what God has given to her for any who have an ear to hear.

For more information, visit her website at kingdompowernow.org.

www.ingramcontent.com/pod-product-compliance
Lightning Source LLC
LaVergne TN
LVHW051055080426
835508LV00019B/1887